L'ANGLAIS
DE LA PSYCHOLOGIE
EN 1000 MOTS

Alain Frangi
Professeur certifié d'anglais
Université René Descartes-Paris V
Christine Roland-Lévy,
Maître de Conférences, psychologue
Université René Descartes-Paris V

BELIN
8, rue Férou, 75006 Paris

Remerciements

Les auteurs tiennent à remercier toute l'équipe du Service d'Anglais pour Psychologues de l'Institut de Psychologie de l'Université René Descartes Paris V et tout particulièrement Marina Bastounis, Maître de Conférences, pour sa lecture attentive et ses remarques constructives.

 ISSN 1240-0793 ISBN 978-2-7011-**1935**-9

Table des matières

Introduction 4

Exercices

1 Historical overview 6

2 Clinical and abnormal psychology 8

3 Cognitive psychology and experimental psychology 11

4 Developmental psychology, child psychology and education 14

5 Differential psychology 17

6 Psychoanalysis 19

7 Psychophysiology 22

8 Social psychology 24

9 Industrial psychology 28

10 Economic psychology 30

11 Statistics and methodology 33

12 General revision 36

Corrigés 40

Lexique anglais-français 46

Lexique français-anglais 72

INTRODUCTION

La collection "en 1000 mots" *s'adresse aux étudiants et aux professionnels qui ont déjà des notions d'une langue étrangère mais ont besoin d'enrichir ou de réviser le vocabulaire de leur domaine.*

ENTRAINEMENT

Des exercices d'entraînement constituent la première partie du livre. Ils vous permettent de contrôler vos connaissances. Les exercices sont groupés par thèmes et les réponses sont données dans le corrigé qui suit.

RÉVISION

Utilisez les lexiques et les exercices pour préparer des examens ou pour rafraîchir votre vocabulaire avant un rendez-vous ou un voyage d'affaires.

LEXIQUES

Le premier lexique (anglais-français) comprend 1000 mots et expressions essentiels de votre spécialité. Le second lexique (français-anglais) est une traduction du premier et vous aidera à retrouver le mot qui vous échappe. Ayez toujours votre livre sur vous pour vérifier rapidement un mot ou une expression.

Attention : *les lexiques ne donnent que les traductions qui concernent la spécialité traitée dans l'ouvrage. Si un mot a plusieurs sens, ils sont donnés à la suite, séparés par des virgules. Si les différents sens sont très éloignés, ils sont séparés par un point-virgule.*

Exercices

1 HISTORICAL OVERVIEW

1 Fill in the blanks in the following text with an appropriate term from the list below.

A. *results* B. *measurement* C. *classify* D. *brains*
E. *experiences* F. *dissecting* G. *approach* H. *daily*
I. *samples* J. *weighing* K. *a series of tests* L. *behaviour*

An attempt was made in earlier times to measure intelligence by (1) .... and (2) .... the brain, but these efforts turned out to be fruitless. No conclusive (3) .... were found as the (4) .... of both genius and idiot were found to be essentially of the same size, weight, and make-up. [...] The first practical (5) .... to the (6) .... of intelligence, made in 1905, is credited to Dr. Alfred Binet. Appointed to study and try to (7) .... bright and dull children, he decided to collect (8) .... of (9) .... in a systematic fashion. Along with other researchers he produced (10) .... derived from the normal (11) .... activities or (12) .... of the child.

2 Replace the words in italics by a term which is more specific.

A. *tasks* B. *ability* C. *score* D. *assumed* E. *the population*
F. *test* G. *average* H. *reliable* I. *development* J. *reasoning*
K. *comprehension* L. *skills* M. *items* N. *standardised*
O. *ratio*

1. Binet (1) *thought* that a dull child was like a normal child, only late in his (2) *growth*.
2. Here are some (3) *elements* from the early (4) *exercise*, showing the various (5) *things* that a French child was expected to do at various ages.
3. The population (6) *mean* for intelligence is 100, and about half of (7) *society* falls within ten points each side

of this middle index score. Does this (8) *number* really represent intelligence?

4. The IQ is an expression of the (9) *proportion* of intelligence to calendar age.
5. Intelligence tests that are (10) *faithful*, valid, and (11) *unchanging* are good tools for measuring mental (12) *capacity*.
6. Mental ability comprises verbal (13) *understanding*, number (14) *counting*, (15) *thinking*, space visualisation, and other problem-solving traits.

3 Match the following words (1-4) to their definitions (a-d).

1. *cybernetics (1948)* 2. *Gestalt (1938)* 3. *Skinner's Box (1951)* 4. *behaviourism (1924)*

A. The subject matter of psychology is the behaviour of human beings.
B. Spatial, visual, auditory and intellectual processes are unities consisting of a whole structure.
C. A device used to study operant conditioning.
D. The comparative study of the automatic control systems formed by the nervous system and brain.

2 CLINICAL AND ABNORMAL PSYCHOLOGY

1 Fill in the blanks in the following text with an appropriate term from the list below.

A. *statistical* B. *psychological* C. *behaviour* D. *cultural* E. *abnormality* F. *concept* G. *healthy* H. *understanding* I. *behaviour* J. *normality*

Abnormality is a derivative (1) .... since it depends on an (2) .... of normality. Moreover, (3) .... describes norms of (4) .... but does not prescribe what is necessarily (5) .... or adaptive. Models of (6) .... have changed over time, from attributing spiritual causes to disorders, to viewing abnormality as erroneous (7) ...., to finally understanding abnormality as involving disorders. Abnormality can be defined and understood in (8) ...., (9) .... and (10) .... terms.

2 Match the elements of therapies that can be linked. Some terms can be used more than once.

1. psychodrama	A. psycho-pharmacology
2. client-centred	B. Gestalt therapy
3. free association	C. cognitive therapy
4. sedatives	D. behaviour therapy
5. operant conditioning	E. shock therapy
6. mood diary	F. Rogerian
7. electro-convulsive shock	G. operant conditioning
8. token economy	H. psychoanalysis
9. benevolent neutrality	I. medical therapy
10. antidepressants	J. humanistic therapy
11. non directive	K. psychotherapy

3 Match the words (1-12) to their French equivalents (a-l).

1. attack	A. bouffée délirante
2. automatic institutionalisation	B. orthophonie
	C. travestissement
3. autoscopic hallucination	D. raptus
4. brief delusional disorder	E. camisole de force
	F. placement d'office
5. clouding	G. confusion mentale
6. factitious disorder	H. ergotherapie
7. speech therapy	I. barrage
8. straight jacket	J. hallucination spéculaire
9. therapy conditioning	
10. thought blocking	K. pathomimie
11. work therapy	L. thérapie par conditionnement
12. cross-dressing	

4 Match the words (1-13) to their definitions (a-m).

1. *agerasia* 2. *acroesthesia* 3. *anhedonia* 4. *aphasia* 5. *anorexia nervosa* 6. *anterograde amnesia* 7. *apraxia* 8. *aprosexia* 9. *asapholalia* 10. *asemia* 11. *astasia-abasia* 12. *hyperphrasia* 13. *alexithymia*

A. Loss of the ability to identify the printed word.
B. Pathologically excessive talking.
C. Inability to stand upright, sit or walk.
D. Inability to understand the meaning of symbols.
E. Poorly articulated speech.
F. Inability to concentrate on things.
G. Inability to perform purposive movements.
H. Loss of memory for events occurring after the causal trauma.
I. Fear of becoming obese (generally unjustified).
J. Partial or complete loss of language abilities.

K. Lack of interest in living and enjoying things.
L. Hypersensitivity in one or more extremities.
M. Vigorous appearance in an older person.

5 Fill in the blanks with the appropriate word in the following list.

A. *aftercare* B. *catchment area* C. *outpatients' department* D. *mood stabiliser* E. *ward* F. *alienated* G. *antidepressant* H. *disorders*

In Great Britain, depressed persons may go to the (1) .... of their (2) ...., where an (3) .... or (4) .... might be prescribed. They will have to return to the same (5) .... regularly for (6) ...., and may never see a severely (7) .... patient in the process; such patients are generally treated in other departments, where more serious (8) .... are dealt with.

6 Match the words (1-10) to their equivalents (a-j).

1. delirious	A. arriération mentale
2. acting out	B. délire
3. borderline *(adj.)*	C. déficit mental
4. mental block	D. pronostic
5. delusion	E. psychasthénie
6. psychoasthenia	F. inhibition
7. forecast	G. passage à l'acte
8. psychasthenia	H. limite
9. arrest	I. délirant
10. mental defect	J. blocage

3 COGNITIVE PSYCHOLOGY AND EXPERIMENTAL PSYCHOLOGY

1 Fill in the blanks in the following text with an appropriate term from the list below.

A. *pause* B. *sample* C. *purpose* D. *results* E. *speakers* F. *deaf* G. *were longer than* H. *normal-hearing* I. *examine*

The (1) .... of Stathopoulos et al. (1986) was to (2) .... the intonations, word durations, and (3) .... durations in the speech of deaf (4) .... They presented some deaf and (5) .... speakers with a short paragraph to be read out loud. This allowed them to use intonation and timing creatively and also provided the authors with comparable speech (6) .... The (7) .... showed that the (8) .... speakers often paused within sentences and that their word durations (9) .... normal hearing speakers.

2 Match the English words on the left (1-14) with their French translations on the right (a-n).

1. training	A. standardiser
2. duration	B. résidu auditif
3. noxious task	C. empan mnésique
4. pitch	D. labyrinthe
5. to standardise	E. rappel
6. loudness	F. lisibilité
7. memory span	G. tonie, hauteur
8. pitch residue	H. sonie
9. readability	I. accentuer
10. rote learning	J. durée
11. maze	K. apprentissage par cœur
12. recall	L. déduire
13. to emphasise	M. formation
14. to infer	N. tâche pénible, désagréable

3 Complete the table below. More than one word can be suggested.

	VERB	NOUN
1.	to assume	
2.		observer
3.	to memorise	
4.		linkage
5.	to reinforce	
6.		experiment
7.	to obey	
8.		learning
9.	to measure	
10.		mediation
11.		research
12.	to differentiate	
13.		procedure
14.		analysis
15.	to bias	

4 Complete the sentences below.

A. *time* B. *predictable* C. *species* D. *chamber* E. *rate* F. *light* G. *device* H. *sound* I. *conditioning* J. *reinforcer* K. *procedures* L. *box* M. *accidental* N. *response* O. *B. F. Skinner*

1. A productive and influential analyst of operant conditioning and reinforcement was ....
2. Though the size and precise content of a Skinner .... vary for different ...., the basic idea remains the same.
3. The animal is put in a .... and ....-proofed ....
4. There is always, within the box, a .... of some sort that the animal can use to elicit a ....

5. The first response is often made as an .... by-product of exploring the box, although shaping .... are often used to encourage that first response.
6. In any event, when the first response is made, it is followed right away by a ....
7. The effect of the reinforcer is .... : the animal tends to repeat the response and thus to get more reinforcers.
8. The basic measure of learning used in operant .... of this kind is the .... of the occurrence of the response over ....

5 Whenever possible, place the words below on Figure 1, and give a short explanation of each.

1. *title* 2. *Y-axis* 3. *X-axis* 4. *legend* 5. *conditions* 6. *three stimuli* 7. *mean time (in minutes)* 8. *days* 9. *results* 10. *conclusions*

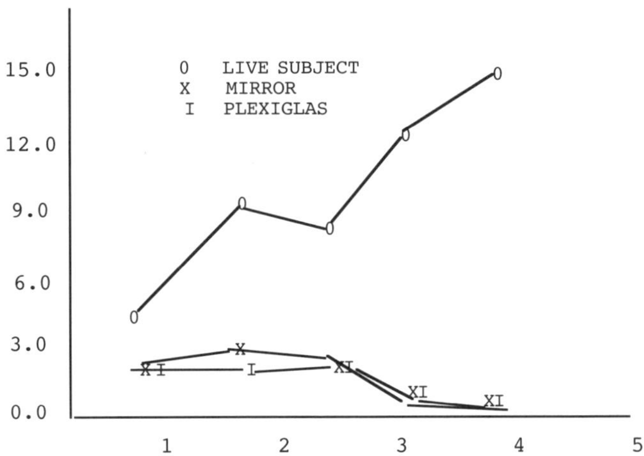

Figure 1.

Mean time spent near a live age mate, or a mirror, or a Plexiglas stimulus object.

4 DEVELOPMENTAL PSYCHOLOGY, CHILD PSYCHOLOGY AND EDUCATION

1 Fill in the blanks in the following text with an appropriate term from the list below.

A. *phenomenon* B. *hypothesis* C. *clusters* D. *different styles* E. *social approval* F. *ability* G. *disapproval* H. *direct reinforcement* I. *emergence* J. *cliques*

Developmental psychologists studying the (1).......... of same-sex preferences in young children offer three (2) .... of explanations for this (3).......... direct reinforcement, cognitive consonance, and behavioural compatibility. The (4) .... hypothesis refers to the possibility that (5) .... from adults or other children for playing with same-sex peers, or (6).......... for playing with opposite-sex peers, underlies same-sex preferences. The second (7) .... also relies on the (8).......... to identify the sex of the partner as well as oneself. Finally, the third hypothesis suggests that boys and girls may segregate into same-sex (9) .... primarily because of differences in their respective behavioural repertoire, or because of their (10).......... of social participation.

2 Match the two parts of the sentences.

1. Records of social behaviour were obtained
2. Approximately two hours of data
3. Data collection procedures involved
4. A minimum of 5-min focal samples
5. Observed social interactions
6. For each observational record the initiator of
7. A 4-item syntax of social exchange is composed of

8. The description of behavioural actions
9. The observational team consisted of

A. were coded as complete sequences.
B. the actor, act, target and target's response.
C. four full-time research personnel.
D. an act as well as the target were noted.
E. using direct-observation procedures.
F. required noting specific behaviours.
G. for each child in the study is needed.
H. obtaining eighty minutes of observation.
I. were available for each individual.

3 Find the English words and their French translations and match them.

1. number conservation
2. age mate
3. conduct
4. acquisition process
5. infant
6. childhood
7. concrete operational stage
8. peer
9. inborn behaviour pattern
10. potential

A. conduite 3
B. pair 8
C. bébé 5
D. stade des opérations concrètes 7
E. comportement inné 9
F. personne du même âge 2
G. potentiel 10
H. processus d'apprentissage 4
I. enfance 6
J. la conservation des nombres 1

4 Match the proper terms to each stage.

1. *conservation* 2. *object permanence* 3. *abstract thinking* 4. *pre-conceptual phase*

A. sensorimotor 2 B. pre-operational stage 4 C. concrete operational stage 1 D. formal operational stage 3

5 Match the different Piagetian stages on the left with the appropriate ages on the right.

1. concrete operational stage
2. pre-operational stage
3. formal operational stage
4. sensorimotor

A. around the age of 12-13
B. from 6-7 to about 12
C. from birth to 2
D. between the ages of 2 to 5-6

6 Match the verbs on the left (1-11) with an appropriate ending on the right (a-k).

1. to punish
2. to play
3. to hide
4. to grasp
5. to be aware
6. to expect
7. to learn
8. to teach
9. to train
10. to reach
11. to follow up

A. a mistake
B. an object
C. a child
D. a role
E. and reappear
F. about conservation of liquids
G. different reactions
H. someone how to manipulate
I. of one's own problems
J. a longitudinal study
K. an operational level

7 Group the 12 words according to the stage (the same 4 stages as in exercise 5) to which they are related.

1. egocentrism
2. operational
3. symbolic schemata
4. concrete
5. hierarchica
6. present-oriented
7. hypothesis testing
8. abstract thinking 3
9. logical reasoning
10. intuitive phase
11. object permanence 4
12. circular reactions

5 DIFFERENTIAL PSYCHOLOGY

1 Fill in the blanks in the following text with an appropriate term from the list below.

A. *variables* B. *observation* C. *purpose* D. *tool* E. *valid* F. *differences* G. *reliable* H. *individuals* I. *standardised* J. *tests*

The (1) .... of differential psychology is to study (2) .... among subjects. Its aim is to compare different conducts and behaviour with objective (3) .... The building of (4) .... which are going to distinguish differences among (5) ...., according to a series of (6) .... (such as sex, age, origins...) will constitute the basis of differential psychology. If the (7) .... to measure the differences is a proper one, it will be (8) ...., (9)............, and (10) ....

2 Find the English words and their French translations and match them.

1. consistency
2. standardised
3. follow-up
4. ranked
5. ability
6. scale
7. valid
8. score
9. sampling
10. reliable
11. rating
12. relevant
13. value

A. ordonné
B. homogénéité
C. capacité
D. standardisé par rapport à un groupe de référence
E. notes, résultats
F. évaluation
G. échantillonnage
H. suivi, étude longitudinale
I. valide
J. échelle
K. fidèle
L. valeur
M. pertinent

3 Match the words (1-10) to their definitions (a-j).

1. *replication* 2. *qualitative difference* 3. *theory* 4. *stimulus* 5. *peer group* 6. *matching* 7. *longitudinal study* 8. *learning set* 9. *control group* 10. *reliability*

A. A group of people like yourself.
B. A study conducted over an extended period of time.
C. The consistency of an event or a measure.
D. A generalised approach to problem-solving: a state of readiness for one kind of solution.
E. Repeating a study, in exactly the same way, the same results should be obtained.
F. Anything which elicits a response of any kind.
G. A group which is used for comparison with an experimental group.
H. A difference in kind, not in amount.
I. Making sure that two sets of experimental materials or subjects are the same in all important aspects.
J. A proposed explanation for an observation or set of observations.

4 Find the complete names of the various tests and include the approximate dates.

TEST	COMPLETE NAME	DATES
WISC		
Stanford-Binet		
WPPSI		
Bailey Mental Scale		
WISC -R		

6 PSYCHOANALYSIS

1 Complete the text with terms from the list below.

A. *psychoanalysis* B. *therapy* C. *neurology* D. *psyche* E. *drives* F. *theory* G. *instincts* H. *disorders* I. *conflicts* J. *treatment*

The Viennese physician Sigmund Freud (1856-1939) developed an early interest in (1) .... into a system of (2) .... for psychological (3) .... His system of (4) .... was known as (5) .... because it emphasised the importance of analysing the (6) .... in order to gain insight into psychological (7) .... Psychoanalysis has also come to be known as a (8) .... of personality and a perspective on human nature. Psychoanalysis assumes that psychological experiences are caused by biological (9) .... and (10) ....

2 Choose the appropriate word from the right-hand column to complete each expression (1-10). Then match the expressions to their translations (I-X).

1. bungled	A. gender
2. discourse	B. memory
3. core	C. stage
4. ego	D. training
5. racial	E. order
6. toilet	F. conflict
7. wish	G. action
8. incest	H. ideal
9. root	I. barrier
10. oral	J. fulfilment

I. *ordre du discours* II. *inconscient collectif* III. *acte manqué* IV. *stade oral* V. *apprentissage de la propreté* VI. *complexe nucléaire* VII. *identité sexuelle* VIII. *barrière de l'inceste* IX. *accomplissement du désir* X. *idéal du moi*

3 Match the words to their definitions.

1. *free association* 2. *re-enactment* 3. *projection* 4. *transference* 5. *Freudian slip* 6. *conversion* 7. *idealised self* 8. *regression* 9. *sublimation* 10. *fixation*

A. Somatisation of psychological maladjustment.

B. A slip of the tongue that is held to reveal some unconscious aspect of the speaker's mind.

C. Redirection of energy from the socially unacceptable to the acceptable.

D. What one would like to become.

E. Unconstrained association made between words, thoughts or ideas.

F. The process by which one's own emotions or feelings are attributed to someone else.

G. Excessive attachment to an object or person that was appropriate for an earlier stage of development.

H. Displacement of feelings applicable toward other persons (parents, spouse…) onto the analyst.

I. Experiencing again the feelings, actions, thoughts or images of an early event in one's life.

J. Flight from reality into a more infantile state.

4 Match the English words on the left with their French equivalents on the right.

1. cathexis	A. culpabilité
2. preconscious	B. répression
3. suppression	C. fratrie
4. parapraxis	D. investissement d'énergie libidinale
5. repression	E. accès de colère
6. unconscious	F. ça
7. guilt	G. acte manqué, lapsus
8. sibship	H. refoulement
9. id	I. inconscient
10. tantrum	J. préconscient

5 Find the terms in the word square which correspond to the following definitions.

1. The set of characteristics which makes each person unique.
2. The third of Freud's psychosexual stages.
3. The conscious element of the psychic apparatus.
4. The first of Freud's psychosexual stages.
5. The part of the psyche, according to Freud, internalising moral and ethical standards.
6. The second of Freud's psychosexual stages.
7. A system of interpreting the mind and behaviour, first developed by Freud.
8. The last of Freud's psychosexual stages in which adult sexuality is assumed.
9. Highly emotional memories.
10. The primitive instinctual element of the psyche, describing the unconscious, according to Freud.
11. The time between age five and puberty.
12. That part of the mind which is not available to conscious scrutiny.

P	S	Y	C	H	O	A	N	A	L	Y	S	I	S
E	G	O	V	Y	R	Z	T	N	E	H	J	D	U
R	B	V	D	O	A	L	P	A	H	G	T	S	P
S	C	V	B	N	L	J	K	L	T	R	Y	E	E
O	B	G	K	P	H	A	L	L	I	C	U	H	R
N	U	N	C	O	N	S	C	I	O	U	S	B	E
A	W	O	R	K	T	R	A	M	A	T	I	B	G
L	A	T	E	N	C	Y	B	R	O	T	H	E	O
I	H	A	R	M	F	U	L	P	L	A	Y	D	R
T	R	A	U	M	A	S	F	R	S	I	O	G	T
Y	C	V	B	N	G	E	N	I	T	A	L	B	G

7 PSYCHOPHYSIOLOGY

1 Complete the diagram using the terms (a-k).

A. *reticular activating system*
B. *pons*
C. *medulla*
D. *corpus callosum*
E. *cerebrum*
F. *pituitary gland*
G. *limbic system*
H. *spinal cord*
I. *cerebellum*
J. *thalamus*
K. *hypothalamus*

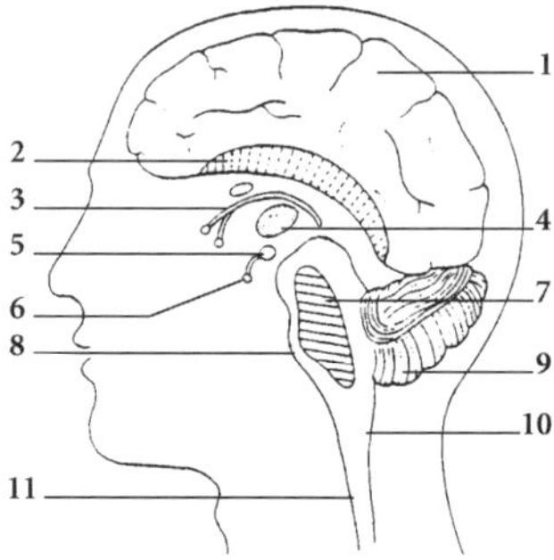

2 Complete the terms, then match them to their translations (I-X).

1. end
2. medulla
3. cerebrospinal
4. pineal
5. cerebellar
6. dura
7. autonomic
8. collateral
9. neural
10. spinal

A. body
B. peduncles
C. mater
D. network
E. button
F. sprouting
G. oblongata
H. cord
I. fluid
J. nervous system

I. épiphyse II. dure-mère III. bouton terminal IV. moëlle épinière V. réseau neuromimétique VI. bulbe rachidien VII. liquide céphalo-rachidien VIII. pédoncules cérébelleux IX. système nerveux végétatif X. surnuméraire collatérale

3 Fill in the blanks with the appropriate term.

A. *lobes* B. *corpus callosum* C. *limbic* D. *pia mater* E. *dura mater* F. *cerebrum* G. *cortex* H. *encephalon* I. *brainstem* J. *pons* K. *fissures* L. *cerebellum* M. *reticular activating system*

The main parts of the (1) .... are: 1. the subcortical structures, i.e. the (2) ...., which links the spinal cord in the backbone with the (3) ...., whose two halves are joined by the (4) .... ; the latter and the (5) .... form the midbrain, above which the hypophysis, hypothalamus and thalamus can be found under the (6) .... system.

The (7) .... consists of two hemispheres linked by the (8) .... and each divided into four (9) .... which are separated by (10) .... The superficial (11) .... is protected by three meninges, the (12) ...., the arachnoid and the (13) ...., the latter next to the skull.

4 Match the expressions (1-6) to their definitions (a-f), then find their French equivalents (I-VI).

1. afferent nerve
2. cable properties
3. cochlea
4. pons
5. efferent nerve
6. fissure

A. Deep groove on the surface of the brain.
B. Collective features of axonal transmission of a neural impulse.
C. Nerve that goes from the periphery toward the central nervous system.
D. Nerve that goes from the brain to the periphery.
E. Rounded prominence on the brainstem.
F. Coiled structure in the inner ear.

I. limaçon II. protubérance annulaire III. scissure IV. caractéristiques normales de l'axone V. nerf sensitif VI. nerf moteur

8 SOCIAL PSYCHOLOGY

1 Fill in the blanks in the following text with an appropriate term from the list below.

A. *society* B. *theory* C. *work* D. *Moscovici* E. *anchoring* F. *individuals* G. *functional* H. *processes* I. *form* J. *objectivation* K. *socially* L. *representations*

Moscovici's (1) .... contains a tension between the functions that social (2) .... serve for (3) ...., and those that they serve for (4) .... as a whole. Indeed, social representations are defined largely in (5) .... terms. Two sets of (6) .... are implied in order to let social representations become generated within a society: (7) .... and (8) .... The content, rather than the (9) ...., of a 'common-sense' is a matter of prime importance, and indeed the focus of most empirical (10) .... that this approach has generated. Such (11) ....-created realities are referred to by (12) .... as 'consensual universe'.

2 Match the words (1-13) to their definitions (a-m).

1. cognitive dissonance
2. control group
3. culture
4. conformity
5. environment
6. feedback
7. cognitive map
8. extraversion
9. interaction
10. concept
11. motivation
12. cross-cultural study
13. norms

A. Information which tells us about the effects of our actions.

B. A mental representation of reality.

C. A set of ideas and properties which can be used to group objects together.

D. The physical and social surroundings of an individual.

E. A group which is used for comparison with an experimental group.

F. The set of accepted ideas, values, and characteristics defining social interaction and practice.

G. A state in which one attitude contradicts another, leading to attitude change.

H. Standards of behaviour which are typical of a society.

I. Doing and thinking what appears to be socially acceptable and prevalent.

J. Reciprocal action, where the actions of one person result in a change in the other's behaviour.

K. That which energises and directs behaviour.

L. A personality trait involving sociability.

M. A comparison of dimensions of social life in different cultural settings.

3 Match each English word or expression (1-10) to its French translation (a-j).

1. peer group
2. in-group
3. prejudice
4. labelling
5. membership
6. role play
7. locus of control
8. residual
9. out-group
10. observer

A. préjugé
B. appartenance
C. groupes de pairs
D. jeu de rôle
E. étiquetage
F. groupe d'appartenance
G. hors-groupe
H. rémanent
I. observateur
J. contrôle interne/externe

4 Make two-word expressions by matching each of the words in the left-hand column (1-14) with the appropriate one in the right-hand column (a-n). Some words can be used more than once.

1. one-way	A. dissonance
2. minority	B. analysis
3. social	C. study
4. free	D. mirror
5. group	E. cultural
6. cross	F. attribution
7. non	G. representation
8. pilot	H. frame
9. cognitive	I. association
10. causal	J. dynamics
11. code	K. influence
12. content	L. directive
13. guide	M. ended
14. open	N. line

5 Put the following steps into a logical order.

1. *results* 2. *dependent variable(s)* 3. *report writing* 4. *discussion* 5. *study design* 6. *hypothesis (hypotheses)* 7. *sample* 8. *theoretical background* 9. *redesign* 10. *procedure* 11. *coding* 12. *communication, publication* 13. *method* 14. *population* 15. *problematics* 16. *literature* 17. *independent variable(s)* 18. *statistical tests* 19. *pre-test* 20. *collecting data*

6 Show that you understand Figure 2 by describing and explaining the following elements.

1. *title* 2. *legend* 3. *Y-axis* 4. *X-axis* 5. *independent variable* 6. *dependent variable* 7. *difference between first rating and second one* 8. *results* 9. *conclusions*

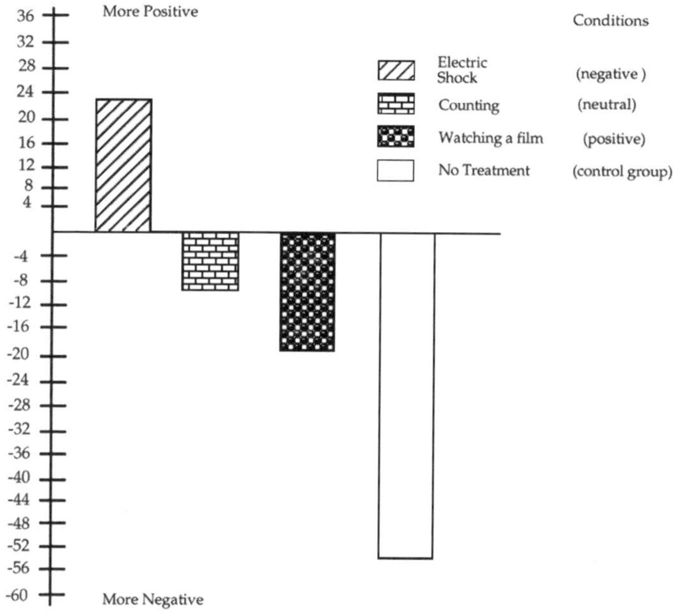

Figure 2 : Change in Rated Attractiveness of Pictures
Second Rating : Difference in mm.

9 INDUSTRIAL PSYCHOLOGY

1 Fill in the blanks in the following text with an appropriate term from the list below.

A. *employee* B. *industrial psychologists* C. *communication* D. *organisational psychologists* E. *workers* F. *leadership* G. *engineering psychology* H. *machines* I. *organisation* J. *applied psychology*

Industrial and organisational psychology, along with engineering and occupational psychology, belong to what is named (1) .... (2) .... work within industrial or employment settings to study and improve the relationship between (3) .... and their jobs and workplace. (4) .... more specifically study the relationship between the (5) .... and his or her employing (6) ...., focusing on group dynamics, (7) ...., management, and (8) .... (9) .... developed as a special application of psychology to the relationship between human workers or equipment operators and the (10) .... and equipment they operate.

2 Match the words (1-8) to their definitions (a-h).

1. organisational psychologists
2. engineering psychology
3. industrial psychology
4. occupational psychiatry
5. applied psychology
6. professional manager
7. human factors psychology
8. ergonomics

A. One who is specifically trained for a managerial position.
B. Field of psychology named after the Greek *ergo* for work because of its applications to work environments.
C. Subdiscipline that focuses on the factors which are important in the person-machine relationship.
D. Field of psychology that studies the person-job interface.
E. Field of psychology studying the interrelationship of humans and machines or equipment.
F. Field of psychiatry concerned with diagnostic and preventive issues within the workplace.
G. Psychologists studying the structure and dynamics of groups and organisations.
H. Psychological theories and research used to solve practical problems.

3 Find the matching terms.

1. expertise	A. «I-O» psychologists
2. field	B. elaborate
3. industrial-organisational	C. function (to)
4. develop	D. plan
5. contribution	E. tutoring
6. operate	F. domain
7. managerial	G. agenda
8. training	H. qualification
9. design	I. professional manager
10. program	J. assistance

10 ECONOMIC PSYCHOLOGY

1 Fill in the blanks in the following text with an appropriate term from the list below.

A. *operations* B. *culture* C. *practice* D. *economic competence* E. *social representations* F. *beliefs* G. *acquisition of knowledge* H. *goals* I. *assimilation* J. *intentions*

The developments that lead to (1) ...., as defined within a particular (2) ...., involve not just the (3) .... that allows the child to undertake these (4) .... It also involves the transmission of an economic identity based on the (5) .... of information, originating from a wide variety of sources, about the acceptable (6) .... of practical action or, in other words, the (7) .... that should govern economic (8) .... In short, knowledge of that which constitutes economic competence in Western societies is gained so that widespread (9) .... about the acceptability of economic goals, or (10) .... of economic actions, come to control the actions of younger members of a society.

2 Match the following words (1-10) to their definitions (a-j).

1. *economic psychology* 2. *personal failure* 3. *saving behaviour* 4. *economic intentions* 5. *debt* 6. *play economy* 7. *economic socialisation* 8. *consumption* 9. *pocket money* 10. *institution*

A. They are constructed within the social group and are realised through practical actions of individuals assisted by the availability of formal institutions or economic facilities.

B. A new interdisciplinary subject which gathers its impetus from the productive association of economics and psychology.

c. Children take part in a broad game using tokens which they have previously earned. The game is structured around aspects of temptation to spend (a sweet shop for example) and threat of losing savings.

d. The act or effect of consuming; the amount consumed.

e. Recent studies have attempted to isolate childhood predictors of adult economic behaviour by relating saving and other financial activities to age, sex, and social class or country.

f. An allowance often given on a weekly/monthly basis.

g. An organisation focused on the promotion of a particular object, e.g. the bank.

h. The act of putting money aside; the conduct implied in not spending.

i. That which is owed; an obligation to make payment in money or kind.

j. A person or a household owing so much money that he or she is in a situation equivalent to bankruptcy.

3 Match the English words and expressions (1-13) to their French equivalents (a-m).

1. consumption	A. emprunter
2. pocket money	B. faillite
3. performance	C. conduite
4. credit	D. consommation
5. to borrow	E. chômage
6. experiment	F. épargne
7. behaviour	G. emploi
8. occupation	H. processus
9. bankruptcy	I. crédit
10. savings	J. compétence
11. unemployment	K. surendettement
12. process	L. argent de poche
13. pluri-indebtedness	M. expérience

4 For each word find the opposite (or nearly opposite) in meaning hidden in the grid.

1. *credit* 2 *pluri-indebtedness* 3. *deficit* 4. *success* 5. *purchase* 6. *corruption* 7. *fair*

A	S	O	S	H	O	N	E	S	T	Y
F	A	L	S	E	L	L	U	R	E	S
F	R	C	R	E	D	I	T	E	S	S
P	U	R	E	S	H	I	L	L	Y	N
A	I	M	F	A	I	L	U	R	E	P
F	R	A	U	D	U	L	E	N	T	Y
C	O	S	A	V	I	N	G	S	U	M
H	O	P	E	S	U	R	P	L	U	S
B	E	L	O	N	T	H	R	I	N	O

5 Join the synonyms (or near synonyms) in the two lists below.

1. exchange	A. failure
2. gain	B. goal
3. saving	C. practical action
4. debt	D. competence
5. credit	E. credence
6. ability	F. due
7. practice	G. economising
8. aim	H. benefit
9. bankruptcy	I. transaction

11 STATISTICS AND METHODOLOGY

1 Fill in the blanks in the following text with an appropriate term.

A. *information* B. *design* C. *results* D. *materials*
E. *replicate* F. *method* G. *apparatus* H. *study*
I. *experiment* J. *subjects* K. *procedure* L. *investigators*

The (1) .... section tells the reader how the (2) .... was conducted. You should include just enough (3) .... so that the reader can (4) .... your (5) .... If you include less information, other (6) .... will be unable to verify your (7) .... The section describing method is usually divided into (8) ...., (9) ...., (10) ...., (11) ...., and (12) ....

2 Match the words (1-11) to their definitions (a-k).

1. *independent variable* 2. *dependent variable* 3. *standard deviation* 4. *range* 5. *procedure* 6. *bar chart* 7. *average* 8. *poll* 9. *references* 10. *abstract* 11. *hypothesis*

A. The literature linked to the topic.

B. It is a measure of the variation in a set of data.

C. It is affected by the other one.

D. A special kind of survey.

E. It is a measure of the spread.

F. It summarises your paper.

G. It is manipulated by the experimenter.

H. The most common expression of the centring of a distribution.

I. A type of graph.

J. The expected link between two types of variables.

K. A chronological account of what happens.

3 Find the English words and their French translations and join them.

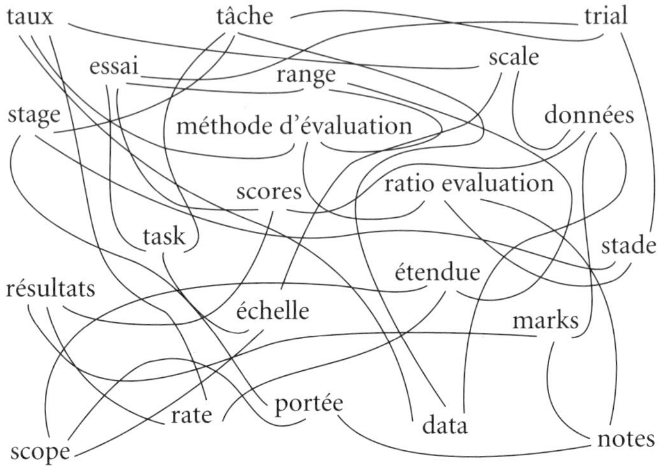

4 What is the plural of the following terms?

1. *hypothesis* 2. *criterion* 3. *phenomenon* 4. *axis* 5. *dotted curve* 6. *bar chart*

5 Are the following statements true (T) or false (F)?

1. The population from which subjects are selected is the population to which the experimental results may be generalised.
2. The subjects who are available usually come from a biased sample of the population from which they are drawn.
3. The materials used in an experiment must be appropriate to the hypothesis under investigation.

4. Statistics deals with techniques for collecting, analysing and drawing conclusions from data.
5. Investigations are often designed to discover and evaluate differences between effects rather than the effects themselves.
6. A computer can make a content analysis.
7. Means and standard deviations are always used to analyse results.
8. Intelligence is distributed like a normal distribution.
9. Computers are clever.
10. A sample consists of a small selection from a larger number of cases about which one intends to gather information.

6 Give the French equivalent of each of the following.

1. *Y-axis* 2. *trial* 3. *trained observer* 4. *task* 5. *random* 6. *learning* 7. *aim* 8. *scatter diagram* 9. *frequency table* 10. *chart* 11. *bar chart*

7 Match the words which are often associated.

1. to administer	A. research
2. interview	B. questions
3. raw	C. a test
4. open-ended	D. guide-lines
5. non-directive	E. control
6. to draw	F. group
7. to test	G. conclusions
8. applied	H. interviews
9. experimental	I. data
10. control	J. a hypothesis

12 GENERAL REVISION

1 Use the definitions to complete the crossword.

ACROSS

1. the act of examining in detail
9. a negative response
10. not to tell the truth
11. to be down in the ....s means to be in a state of depression
13. a Freudian .... may reveal an unconscious aspect of your mind
14. to place inside
16. alternatively
17. investigatory studies
20. primitive conscious elements
21. to leave out
24. I had to refer .... a previous study.
26. that is to say *(Latin)*
27. Unconditioned Stimulus
28. anxiety generated by desire
29. the basis of measurement *(plural)*
31. conclusions are based .... results
32. The results were not as conclusive .... had been hoped.
33. the opposite of 'borrowed'
37. level, step
38. an instrument to measure a factor or assess an ability

DOWN

1. single person, animal or thing
2. the part of speech which may be the subject of a verb
3. research methods
4. plural of 38 across
5. any instrument or device designed to facilitate running an experiment

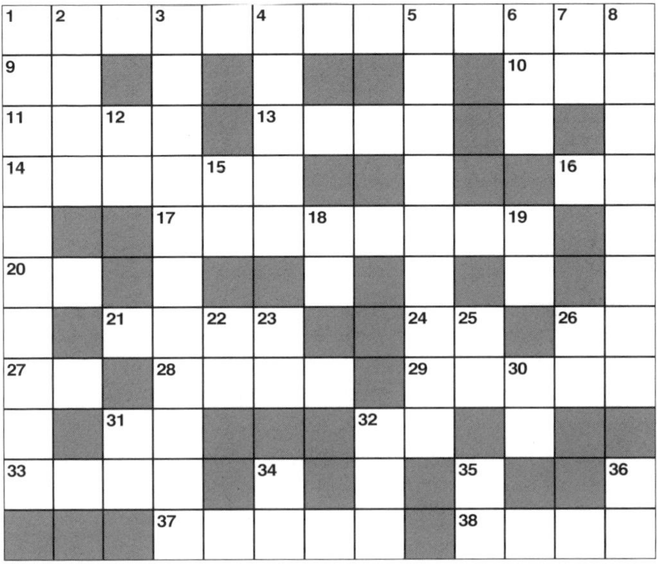

6. not well mentally, sick
7. Observed Interaction
8. basic structural and functional units of the nervous system
12. Multiple Sclerosis
15. with reference to
18. for example *(Latin)*
19. the subject pronoun that designates the male
22. The interviews took place .... the street.
23. television *(abbreviation)*
25. The results could be seen clearly .... the graph.
26. the personal pronoun designating an inanimate object
30. Intelligence Quotient
31. He put .... a smile to cover his embarrassment.
32. She is thirty-five but has a mental .... of ten.
34. Master of Arts
35. the same as 26 down
36. He qualified as a psychologist .... the end of the course.

2 Put the following sentences in a logical order (from 1 to 9). The result will give you information on how to structure an abstract.

1. The abstract, like the title, should be self-explanatory and self-contained, because it is used for indexing by information-retrieval networks.

2. Do not include in the abstract any information that is not included in the body of the paper.

3. Remember that most people will read your abstract only if your title interests them and will accept and read your article only if your abstract interests them.

4. Because you will not know until you are done with the outline what information you will include, you are well advised to defer writing the abstract until after you have otherwise completed the outline, or even the paper itself.

5. Its length should be of approximately 10 to 20 lines: 100-150 words for a report of an empirical study and 75-100 words for a theoretical article or literature review.

6. It is therefore essential that the abstract interests your reader.

7. The abstract should include (a) the major hypotheses, (b) a summary of the method, including a description of the materials, apparatus, subjects, design, and procedure, (c) a synopsis of the main results and (d) the conclusions drawn from the results.

8. The abstract summarises your paper.

9. You can interest the reader by showing that the problem is an important one, that your hypotheses about the problem are insight-full ones and that you will test these hypotheses in a convincing way.

Corrigés

1 HISTORICAL OVERVIEW
(pages 6 et 7)

1 1-J, 2-F, 3-A, 4-D, 5-G, 6-B, 7-C, 8-I, 9-L, 10-K, 11-H, 12-E.

2 1-D, 2-I, 3-M, 4-F, 5-A, 6-G, 7-E, 8-C, 9-O, 10-H, 11-N, 12-B, 13-K, 14-L, 15-J.

3 1-D, 2-B, 3-C, 4-A.

2 CLINICAL AND ABNORMAL PSYCHOLOGY (pages 8 à 10)

1 1-F, 2-H, 3-J, 4-C, 5-G, 6-E, 7-I, 8/9/10-A/D/B (8, 9 and 10 are in a logical order, but it could be different).

2 (other links can be made, but these are the most obvious) 1-B, 2-F, 3-H, 4-A, 5-D, 6-C, 7-E, 8-G, 9-K, 10-I, 11-J.

3 1-D, 2-F, 3-J, 4-A, 5-G, 6-K, 7-B, 8-E, 9-L, 10-I, 11-H, 12-C.

4 1-M, 2-L, 3-K, 4-J, 5-I, 6-H, 7-G, 8-F, 9-E, 10-D, 11-C, 12-B, 13-A.

5 1-C, 2-B, 3-G, 4-D, 5-E, 6-A, 7-F, 8-H.

6 1-I, 2-G, 3-H, 4-J, 5-B, 6-A, 7-D, 8-E, 9-F, 10-C.

3 COGNITIVE PSYCHOLOGY AND EXPERIMENTAL PSYCHOLOGY
(pages 11 à 13)

1 1-C, 2-I, 3-A, 4-E, 5-H, 6-D, 7-B, 8-F, 9-G.

2 1-M, 2-J, 3-N, 4-G, 5-A, 6-H, 7-C, 8-B, 9-F, 10-K, 11-D, 12-E, 13-I, 14-L.

3 1. assumption 2. to observe 3. memory 4. to link 5. reinforcement 6. to experiment 7. obedience 8. to learn 9. measurement 10. to mediate 11. to research 12. differentiation 13. to proceed 14. to analyse 15. bias

4 1-O, 2-L-C, 3-F-H-D, 4-G-N, 5-M-K, 6-J, 7-B, 8-I-E-A.

5 1. Mean time spent near a live age mate, a mirror, or a Plexiglas stimulus object 2. mean time in minutes 3 days 4. Live subject 0, Mirror X, Plexiglas I 5. there are 3 conditions, one for each stimulus (Live subject, Mirror, Plexiglas) 6. Live subject, Mirror, Plexiglas 7. on the Y-axis (0.0, 3.0, 6.0, 9.0, 12.0, 15.0) 8. on the X-axis : 5 days (1, 2,

3, 4, 5) **9.** there is a significant ($p<.05$) Days by Stimulus object interaction **10.** the live age mate was always preferred

4 DEVELOPMENTAL PSYCHOLOGY, CHILD PSYCHOLOGY AND EDUCATION (pages 14 à 16)

1 1-I, 2-C, 3-A, 4-H, 5-E, 6-G, 7-B, 8-F, 9-J, 10-D.

2 1-E, 2-I, 3-H, 4-G, 5-A, 6-D, 7-B, 8-F, 9-C.

3 1-J, 2-F, 3-A, 4-H, 5-C, 6-I, 7-D, 8-B, 9-E, 10-G.

4 1-C, 2-A, 3-D, 4-B.

5 1-B, 2-D, 3-A, 4-C.

6 1-A, 2-D, 3-E, 4-B, 5-I, 6-G, 7-F, 8-H, 9-C, 10-K, 11-J.

7 egocentrism/object permanence/circular reactions, operational/symbolic schemata/intuitive phase, concrete/hierarchical/present-oriented, abstract thinking/logical reasoning/hypothesis testing

5 DIFFERENTIAL PSYCHOLOGY (pages 17 et 18)

1 1-C, 2-F, 3-B, 4-J, 5-H, 6-A, 7-D, 8/9/10-G/I/E (in any order).

2 1-B, 2-D, 3-H, 4-A, 5-C, 6-J, 7-I, 8-E, 9-G, 10-K, 11-F, 12-M, 13-L.

3 1-E, 2-H, 3-J, 4-F, 5-A, 6-I, 7-B, 8-D, 9-G, 10-C.

4 **1.** WISC = Wechsler Intelligence Scale for Children **2.** Stanford-Binet (1972) **3.** WPPSI = Wechsler Preschool and Primary Scale of Intelligence (1967) **4.** Bayley Scale of Infant Development (1969) **5.** WISC-R.= Wechsler Intelligence Scale for Children-Revised in 1974.

6 PSYCHOANALYSIS (pages 19 à 21)

1 1-C, 2-J, 3-H, 4-B, 5-A, 6-D, 7-I, 8-F, 9-E (OR G), 10-G (OR E).

2 1-G-III, 2-E-I, 3-A-VII, 4-H-X, 5-B-II, 6-D-V, 7-J-IX, 8-I-VIII, 9-F-VI, 10-C-IV.

3 1-E, 2-I, 3-F, 4-H, 5-B, 6-A, 7-D, 8-J, 9-C, 10-G.

4 1-D, 2-J, 3-B, 4-G, 5-H, 6-I, 7-A, 8-C, 9-F, 10-E.

5 HORIZONTAL: psychoanalysis (7), ego (3), phallic (8), unconscious (12), latency (11), traumas (9), genital (2).

VERTICAL: personality (1), oral (4), anal (6), id (10), superego (5).

7 PSYCHOPHYSIOLOGY

(pages 22 et 23)

1 1-E, 2-D, 3-G, 4-J, 5-K, 6-F, 7-A, 8-B, 9-I, 10-C, 11-H.

2 1-E-III, 2-G-VI, 3-I-VII, 4-A-I, 5-B-VIII, 6-C-II, 7-J-IX, 8-F-X, 9-D-V, 10-H-IV.

3 1-H, 2-I, 3-L, 4-M, 5-J, 6-C, 7-F, 8-B, 9-A, 10-K, 11-G, 12-E, 13-D.

4 1-C-V, 2-B-IV, 3-F-I, 4-E-II, 5-D-VI, 6-A-III.

8 SOCIAL PSYCHOLOGY

(pages 24 à 27)

1 1-B, 2-L, 3-F, 4-A, 5-G, 6-H, 7-E (OR J), 8-J (OR E), 9-I, 10-C, 11-K, 12-D.

2 1-G, 2-E, 3-F, 4-I, 5-D, 6-A, 7-B, 8-L, 9-J, 10-C, 11-K, 12-M, 13-H.

3 1-C, 2-F, 3-A, 4-E, 5-B, 6-D, 7-J, 8-H, 9-G, 10-I.

4 (This is one possibility. Other combinations are possible.) 1-D, 2-K, 3-G, 4-I, 5-J, 6-E, 7-L, 8-C, 9-A, 10-F, 11-H, 12-B, 13-N, 14-M.

5 16, 8, 15, 6, 17, 2, 13, 14, 10, 5, 7, 19, 9, 20, 11, 18, 1, 4, 3, 12.

6 1. Change in rated attractiveness of pictures. 2. Four conditions: electric shock (negative), counting (neutral), watching a film (positive), no treatment (control group). 3. Difference, in millimetres (from - 60 to + 36), between a first rating and a second one. 4. Results obtained for each condition (bars). 5. Four conditions, from positive to negative, passing by neutral and no treatment. 6. Change in rated attractiveness (difference between ratings in millimetres). 7. From - 60 to + 36 millimetres. 8. The negative condition influences the second evaluation in a positive direction; all the other situations have a negative effect on the second evaluation. 9. The neutral condition should produce no difference (0 mm); the no treatment situation

produces the largest difference, towards a more negative second evaluation, which implies a positive situation in the so-called «no treatment» condition.

9 INDUSTRIAL PSYCHOLOGY
(pages 28 et 29)

1 1-J, 2-B, 3-E, 4-D, 5-A, 6-I, 7-F, 8-C, 9-G, 10-H.

2 1-G, 2-E, 3-D, 4-F, 5-H, 6-A, 7-C, 8-B.

3 1-H, 2-F, 3-A, 4-B, 5-J, 6-C, 7-I, 8-E, 9-D, 10-G.

10 ECONOMIC PSYCHOLOGY
(pages 30 à 32)

1 1-D, 2-B, 3-G, 4-A, 5-I, 6-H, 7-J, 8-C, 9-F, 10-E.

2 1-B, 2-J, 3-H, 4-A, 5-I, 6-C, 7-E, 8-D, 9-F, 10-G.

3 1-D, 2-L, 3-J, 4-I, 5-A, 6-M, 7-C, 8-G, 9-B, 10-F, 11-E, 12-H, 13-K.

4 1. savings 2. credit 3. surplus 4. failure 5. sell 6. honesty 7. fraudulent.

5 1-I, 2-H, 3-G, 4-F, 5-E, 6-D, 7-C, 8-B, 9-A.

11 STATISTICS AND METHODOLOGY
(pages 33 à 35)

1 1-F, 2-I, 3-A, 4-E, 5-H, 6-L, 7-C, 8-D, 9-G, 10-J, 11-B, 12-K.

2 1-G, 2-C, 3-E, 4-B, 5-K, 6-I, 7-H, 8-D, 9-A, 10-F, 11-J.

3 data/données, marks/notes, scores/résultats, stage/stade, scale/échelle, rate/taux, scope/portée, ratio evaluation/méthode d'évaluation, range/étendue, trial/essai, task/tâche.

4 1. hypotheses 2. criteria 3. phenomena 4. axes 5. dotted curves 6. bar charts

5 1-T, 2-T, 3-T, 4-T, 5-T, 6-T, 7-F, 8-T, 9-F, 10-T.

6 1. ordonnée 2. essai 3. observateur formé 4. tâche 5. aléatoire 6. l'apprentissage 7. but 8. nuage de points 9. tableau de fréquences 10. graphique 11. histogramme

7 1-C, 2-D, 3-I, 4-B, 5-H, 6-G, 7-J, 8-A, 9-E, 10-F.

12 GENERAL REVISION
(pages 36 à 38)

1 ACROSS: **1.** investigation **9** no **10.** lie **11.** dump **13.** slip **14.** insert **16.** or **17.** research **20.** id **21.** omit **24.** to **26.** i.e. **27.** US **28.** envy **29.** units **31.** on **32.** as **33.** lent **37.** stage **38.** test

DOWN: **1.** individual **2.** noun **4.** experiments **5.** apparatus **6.** ill **7.** OI **8.** neurones **12.** MS **15.** re **18.** e.g. **19.** he **22.** in **23.** TV **25.** on **26.** it **30.** IQ **31.** on **32.** age **34.** MA **35.** it **36.** at

2 8, 5, 1, 7, 2, 4, 3, 6, 9.

VOCABULAIRE ANGLAIS-FRANÇAIS

A

abandonment complex abandonnisme
abatement diminution
abient behaviour évitement
ability capacité ; facteur
abnormal psychology psychopathologie
abreaction abreaction
absent-mindedness distraction
absolute threshold seuil absolu
absolutism absolutisme
abstract abstrait ; synthèse *(n.)*
abulia aboulie
abulic aboulique
acathexis non-investissement
accelerated speech logorrhée
accurate exact, précis
achieved status statut acquis
achievement réussite, performance
  achievement motive mobile de réussite
  achievement need besoin de performance
  achievement quotient / test /quotient /test d'instruction
acouasma acouasmie
acousma acousmie
acquired acquis
acquisition acquisition ; apprentissage
acquisitiveness avidité
acroesthesia acroesthésie
acting-out passage à l'acte
activated sleep sommeil agité
activity box cage d'activité
actual neurosis névrose actuelle
actualising actualisation
  actualising tendency réalisation de soi
adaptive adapté
addict toxicomane
addicted dépendant
addiction dépendance, assuétude ; toxicomanie
adduced invoqué
adequate adapté, convenable
adhesiveness viscosité
adient behaviour approche
adipsia adipsie
adjusted adapté
adjustment adaptation
adrenal gland glande surrénale
adult unsound of mind incapable majeur
advantage by illness bénéfice de la maladie
adventitious reinforcement renforcement fortuit, aléatoire
affect states états affectifs
affective flattening indifférence affective
affective schizophrenia psychose dysthymique
afferent system afférence
affiliation appartenance
after-discharge post-décharge, décharge consécutive
after-effect effet consécutif
after-image rémanence
aftercare postcure
age mate sujet du même âge
ageism âgisme
agency instance *(notamment : censure)*
agenesis agénésie
agerasia agérasie
aggregate ensemble ; total
aggressiveness agressivité
aha *(reaction, experience)* intuition soudaine
ahypnia, ahypnosia insomnie
AI (Artificial Intelligence) intelligence artificielle
aim but ; visée ; objectif
  aim-inhibition inhibition d'aspiration
alallia aphasie fonctionnelle
alertness tonus
alexithymia alexithymie
algophilia masochisme, algophilie
all-or-none principle principe du tout ou rien
alleviation soulagement
allotriophagy parorexie

altercasting incitation individuelle *(jeu de rôle)*
alternate-form (reliability/tests) (fidélité) par équivalence ; (tests) parallèles
alternating response alternance
alternation alternance
ambient physical factor ambiance physique
amino acids acides aminés
anaclisis étayage ; dépendance émotionnelle
anaclitic depression dépréssion anaclitique
analysand analysant *(en analyse didactique)*
analysis (*pl.* analyses) analyse
multivariate analysis analyse multivariée
scale analysis analyse hiérarchique
analyst analyste
anchor effect effet d'ancrage
anchor point point de référence
anchoring ancrage
anguish angoisse
anhedonia anhédonie
anorexia nervosa anorexie mentale
anterograde amnesia amnésie anterograde, amnésie de fixation
anticathexis contre-investissement
antidepressant antidépresseur
anxiety anxiété ; angoisse
aphasia aphasie
apparatus appareil(s), appareillage, dispositif
appeal attrait
apperception identification ; a(p)perception
applied appliqué
applied psychology psychologie appliquée
appoint (to) nommer (à un poste)
appraisal expertise ; évaluation
approval approbation
apraxia apraxie
aprosexia aprosexie
aptitude test test d'aptitude
Artificial Intelligence (AI) intelligence artificielle
arousal activation, (réaction d') éveil, excitation
array flux (optique) ; environnement *(visuel)*
arrest inhibition
artefact artéfact ; biais
asapholalia asapholalie
ascendance ascendant *(n.)*
ascribed status statut attribué
asemia asémie
asocial asocial
assertiveness affirmation de soi , assertivité
assess (to) évaluer, estimer
assessment évaluation, estimation
assignment placement, répartition ; consigne
association network réseau d'association
assume (to) supposer
assumption supposition, présupposé
astasia-abasia astasie-abasie
asthenia asthénie
astraphobia astraphobie
asylum asile
ataractic imperturbable *(patient)* ; calmant *(médicament)*
ataxia ataxie
attachment attachement
attack raptus
attainment obtention, réalisation
attempt essai ; tentative
attensity attensité
attention seeking captativité, recherche d'attention
attention-deficit disorder troubles de l'attention
attic child enfant reclus, enfant du placard
attitude scale échelle d'attitudes
attribute (to) attribuer
attribution attribution
audile auditif *(n.)*
auditory area aire d'audition

auditory flutter alternance sonore périodique
autism autisme
autistic *(adj.)* autiste
autogenic autogène
automatic institutionalisation placement d'office
autonomic conditioning conditionnement des fonctions involontaires
autonomic nervous system système nerveux végétatif
autoscopic hallucination hallucination spéculaire
auto-sensuous (*Tustin*) autosensuel, autiste normal
average moyen, ordinaire *(adj.)* ; moyenne *(n.)*
  average deviation écart moyen
avoidance évitement
aware conscient *(vigilant)*
awareness (prise de) conscience ; avertissement *(Rogers)*
axis (*pl.* **axes**) axe *(abstrait)*
axle axe *(concret)*
axon axone

B

babble babil, gazouillement
baby-talk imitation par l'adulte de l'élocution infantile
backward rétrograde ; arriéré
backwardness arriération
balance équilibre ; équilibration
  balance experience résonance intime *(Rorschach)*
bandwagon effect conformisme grégaire
bankruptcy faillite
barbiturate barbiturique
bar chart histogramme
barrier barrière
basal ganglia noyaux gris centraux
base rate fréquence normale d'occurence par unité de temps
baseline frequency fréquence normale
basic fault défaut fondamental
basic mistrust méfiance fondamentale
battered *(wife, child...)* battu
battery sévices
bedlam asile d'aliénés
bedwetting énurésie
behavior *(US)*, **behaviour** *(UK)* comportement
  adient behaviour approche
  behaviour setting cadre comportemental
  dissociative behaviour comportement dissocié
  respondent behaviour comportement opérant
behavioristics science du comportement
behavioural comportemental
belief system système de croyances
belief-value matrix matrice croyance-valeur
belongingness (sentiment d') appartenance
beneceptor récompense
beneffectance tendance à valoriser son rôle dans les événements positifs et le minimiser dans ceux qui sont négatifs
benevolent neutrality neutralité bienveillante
bereavement deuil ; perte
between-brain diencéphale
between-group inter-groupe
bias (to) fausser, biaiser
  biased scanning biais d'examen
bias biais
bigoted sectaire, fanatique
bilingual bilingue
bilingualism bilinguisme
binaural shift son binaural glissant
bionics bionique *(n.)*
bipolar disorder état mixte
bisected brain cerveau séparé
black box boîte noire
blackout perte de conscience *(notamment coma éthylique)*
blank piège *(expériences)* ; espace blanc *(tests)*

blind alley cul-de-sac
blind analysis analyse aveugle
block, blocking blocage
blood pressure tension artérielle
blood type groupe sanguin
blood-brain barrier barrière (hémato-)méningée
blunted affect émoussement affectif
body ego moi corporel
body image image corporelle
body language langage gestuel
bond lien
bonding lien socio-émotionnel
borderline état-limite ; zone marginale
  borderline psychosis prépsychose
bottom-down/-up descendant, ascendant
boundary frontière
brain cerveau, encéphale
brainstem bulbe rachidien, tronc cérébral
brainstorming assaut d'idées
breakdown effondrement
breaking up démantèlement
breakthrough insight
brief delusional disorder bouffée délirante aigüe (BDA)
brief reactive psychosis bouffée délirante réactionnelle
bulimia boulimie
bundle faisceau de nerfs ; volée d'influx
  bundle hypothesis hypothèse structuraliste *(Gestalt)*
bungled action acte manqué
burn-out syndrome d'épuisement professionnel (SEP)
burst of tone bouffée de son
buzzer sonnette, signal, "trembleur"
by-product artefact erreur de mesure
bystander apathy indifférence du spectateur

C

candid sincère
capacity for concern capacité de sollicitude
capacity for reform amendabilité
CAT (**Children's Apperception Test**) CAT
CAT (**Computerized Axial Tomography**) scannographie
catchment area secteur
catharsis catharsis
cathect (to) investir
cathection investissement
cathexis investissement ; cathexis *(Tolman)* ; énergie
caudate nucleus noyau caudé
cell bodies corps cellulaires
censorship censure
centering *(US)*, **centring** *(UK)* centrage
central nervous system système nerveux central
cerebellar cerebelleux
cerebellum cervelet
cerebral palsy infirmité motrice cérébrale
chart graphique
check (to) vérifier ; cocher *(case)*
chemically-gated à ouverture chimique
chemotherapy chimiothérapie
Children's Apperception Test (CAT) CAT
chi-square khi-deux, khi-carré
chromaticity coordinates coordonnées trichromatiques
chromaticness chromie
chronological age âge réel
chunk agrégat codé
chunking fragmentation, regroupement
clang association similarité de son ; test de rime
clearing dégagement *(psychan.)*
client-cent(e)red centré sur le client
climacteric ménopause ; andropause

clinic clinique *(n.)*
clinical clinique *(adj.)*
closing-in accolement au modèle
closure clôture, structuration perceptive
clouding of consciousness confusion mentale
cloze procedure test lacunaire
clue indice, guide, fil conducteur
cluster grappe, groupe, groupement ; cluster, arborescence
co-twins co-jumeaux
co-twin control homozygote témoin
coach (to) guider, entraîner
coaching formation *(lors d'un test)*
cochlea limaçon
code switching alternance de codes
coding codage
cognitive dissonance dissonance cognitive
cognitive heterogeneity dysharmonie cognitive pathologique
cognitive mapping mise en carte cognitive
cognise (to) savoir ; penser
cohesiveness cohésion
cohort cohorte ; groupe, catégorie, classe d'âge
cohort effect effet de génération
coition, coitus coït
collateral sprouting surnuméraire collatérale
collect (to) réunir
collective unconscious inconscient collectif
colour blindness daltonisme
commit (to) interner
compensating compensatoire
completion test test lacunaire
compliance soumission, complaisance
compound composé, complexe
compulsion compulsion ; contrainte
Computerised Axial Tomography (CAT) scannographie
conclusive concluant, probant
concrete operations (stade des) opérations concrètes *(Piaget)*
concreteness concrétude
conditioned reinforcer renforcement secondaire/conditionné
conditioning conditionnement
confederate compère, complice, comparse
confidence confiance
confounding confusionnel
confounding variable variable dont l'effet ne peut pas être mesuré indépendamment de celui d'une autre variable
confusion scales échelles cumulatives
congruity congruence
connate congénital, prénatal
connectedness connexité
conscience conscience (morale)
conscious conscient *(adj. & n.)*
conscious scheme organisation consciente
consciousness conscience *(état conscient)*
consistency constance ; cohérence ; *(psychométrie)* fidélité , homogénéité ; consistance ; logique
constancy constance
constraint contrainte
construct construit, concept *(ex : test de Kelly)* ; construction mentale, construct
consume consommer
consummatory consommatoire
consummatory act acte consommatoire
consumption consommation
content analysis analyse de contenu
contingent reinforcement renforcement dépendant
contrectation caresses sexuelles
control group groupe témoin
converse inverse
conversion conversion
convolution circonvolution
convulsant convulsivant

cooing gazouillis *(de bébé)*
corpora quadrigemina tubercules quadrijumeaux
corpus callosum corps calleux
corpus striatum corps strié
cortical inhibitory control frein cortical
cot death mort subite du nourrisson
counterbalanced order ordre de contrebalancement
courtship cour, parade amoureuse
covert caché, interne ; implicite
craving manque (de drogue)
crisis (*pl.* **crises**) crise
criterion (*pl.* **criteria**) critère
  criterion group groupe d'étalonnage
critic critique *(personne)*
critical critique *(adj.)* ; discriminant
critique, criticism critique *(évaluation)*
cross-cultural interculturel
cross-dressing travestissement
cross-hearing audition transcrânienne
cross-modal intermodal
  cross-modal sensory integration coordination intersensorielle
cross-section coupe transversale ; groupe représentatif
cross-sectional transversal
cross-sequential transversal-séquentiel
cross-validation validation croisée, contre-validation
crude brut *(stat.)*
crystallised intelligence intelligence cristallisée
cue indice, signe, repère
  cue-stimulus stimulus discriminatif
cultural conserve rôle stéréotypé
cultural lag décalage culturel
culture-free test/-fair test test indépendant de la culture
cyclothymic cyclothymique

D

damming up stase *(libidinale)*
datum (*pl.* **data**) donnée
dazzlemeter caliginimètre
De Clérambault's syndrome automatisme mental
de-adaptation désadaptation
dead end cul-de-sac
deafness surdité
death wish pulsion de mort
decathect (to) désinvestir
decathection désinvestissement
decentering *(US)*, **decentring** *(UK)* décentrage, décalage
decrement diminution
decussation décussation
defence *(UK)*, **defense** *(US)* défense
deferred après-coup
deficiency carence, déficit fonctionnel
deflection déviation, déflexion
defusion désintrication
degeneration dégénérescence
degree degré ; diplôme
  degree of freedom degré de liberté
delayed reaction réaction conditionnelle, réaction différée
delirious délirant ; confuso-onirique
delove désamour
delusion délire ; délusion
delusional, delusionary délirant
  delusional imagination délire d'imagination
dendrite dendrite
denial déni
dependency needs besoins vitaux
dependent variable variable dépendante
depression dépression
  anaclitic depression dépréssion anaclitique
deprivation privation
dereistic déréel, déréistique
derivative (of the unconscious) rejeton (de l'inconscient)

descriptive unconscious préconscient
desensitisation désensibilisation
design plan
destructuralisation déstructuration
detection dépistage
develop (to) élaborer, développer ; évoluer
developmental psychology psychologie génétique/ du développement
deviate déviant
deviation écart
diagnose (to) diagnostiquer
diagnosis (*pl.* **diagnoses**) diagnostic
diaphoresis transpiration abondante
diary journal
difference limen/threshold échelon/seuil différentiel
differentiate différencier
digit-span test test arithméthique de rappel
dilemma dilemne
dimming effect effet d'assombrissement
diplacusis diplacousie
diplegia hémiplégie
disability incapacité
disabled handicapé, infirme
disablement invalidité
disapproval désapprobation
disavowal déni ; reniement, désaveu
discrete distinct ; discontinu
discriminal discriminatif
discriminating fineness sensibilité (de tests)
discriminating power pouvoir classant
disfluency difficulté(s) d'élocution
dishabituation déshabituation
disorder trouble
displacement déplacement
displacement activities activités de déplacement, activités redirigées
display signal ; exposition, présentation ; *(éthol.)* prestance
display rule règle spécifique d'émission
dissect (to) disséquer
dissociative behaviour comportement dissocié
distinctiveness degré de séparabilité ; caractéristique distinctive
distraction confusion ; distraction
disuse non-usage
dizygotic hétérozygote *(voir DZA)*
doodle gribouillage
dotted en pointillé
double-barrelled question question à double implication
double-bind double lien / contrainte
Down's syndrome trisomie 21 *(mongolisme)* ; trisomique *(mongolien)*
drift dérive
drive pulsion, tension ; mobile, motivation *(Hull)* ; (maternal) instinct ; besoin, tendance impulsive
drive derivative dérivé pulsionnel
drug médicament ; drogue
DSM «Manuel statistique et diagnostique des troubles mentaux»
dual double, duel
dual personality dédoublement de la personnalité
dull terne, ennuyeux ; stupide ; rebattu *(couleur d'objet)*
dumb muet ; stupide
dummy placebo
dyad dyade
dysconnection déconnexion
dysfunction désordre, dysfonctionnement
dyslexia dyslexie
dysthymia dysthymie
DZA (DiZygotic twins raised Apart) hétérozygotes élevés séparément

E

earliness précocité
eccentric excentrique
economise (to) épargner
educational age âge d'acquisition
EEG électro-encéphalogramme
effective time temps utile
efferent system éfference
ego moi
  body ego moi corporel
  ego ideal idéal du moi
  ego splitting clivage du moi
  ego-involvement engagement du moi
  ego-relatedness relation au moi
  ideal ego moi idéal
egocentrism égocentrisme
egoism égoïsme
egoist *(n.)*, **egoistic** *(adj.)* égoïste
egotism vanité
egotistic(al) vaniteux
eidetic imagery mémoire photographique
elation exaltation
electroplexy sismothérapie
elicit a response (to) provoquer/entraîner une réponse
ellipsis (*pl.* ellipses) ellipse
elopement évasion *(d'une institution psychiatrique)*
embedded figures figures intriquées
embedding encastrement
emergence apparition
emote (to) s'émouvoir
emotional émotionnel, affectif
  emotional deprivation carence affective
  emotional tone coloration affective
emotionalism émotivité
emphasis (*pl.* **emphases**) accentuation, force
emphasise (to) mettre l'accent sur, mettre en valeur
empiricism empirisme
enactive representation représentation d'actions
encephalon encéphale
encopresis incontinence fécale, encoprésie
end-button/-foot bouton terminal
endbrain télencéphale
ending terminaison (nerveuse)
endo-cathection investissement interne
endocrine glands glandes endocrines
engineering psychology psychologie de l'ingénierie
engram engramme
enquiry recherche, investigation
entropy entropie
enuresis énurésie
environment milieu
epidemic épidémie
epilepsy épilepsie
equal/equivalent loudness isotonie
equilibrium équilibre
equivalent test test parallèle
ergonomics ergonomie
eroticisation érotisation
escape échappement
estimation estimation
eveningness vespéralité
eviration castration ; délire d'un homme croyant s'être transformé en femme
ex post facto rétrospectif
excitatory excitatif
exhibitionism besoin d'attirer l'attention ; *(paraphilie)* exhibitionnisme
exocathection investissement externe
expectancy expectation ; espérance (de vie)
expectation attente ; prévision
experience expérience *(vécue)* ; le vécu
experiment expérience *(scientifique)*
experimental design plan d'expérience
experimental group groupe expérimental

experimental paradigm procédure expérimentale, paradigme
experimenter expérimentateur
expert expert ; juge
expertise connaissances techniques, savoir-faire
exposition need besoin d'expliquer
expressive aphasia aphasie de Broca
extrajection projection
extraneous accessoire, extérieur *(adj.)*
extrinsic extrinsèque
extroversion extraversion, extroversion
extrovert extraverti
eye-blink réflexe palpébral
eye movement oculomotricité
eye-span champ visuel
eye-speech span écart oculo-verbal
eyedness ocularité

F

fabrication fabulation, invention
facial feedback réverbération faciale
facilitation facilitation ; frayage
factitious disorder pathomimie
factor facteur
  factor analysis of correspondence analyse factorielle des correspondances
  factor measurement mesure en facteur
  factor score note en facteur
fading altération, affaiblissement
failure défaillance ; échec, faillite
fair honnête ; juste, équitable
faithful fidèle
fallacy faux raisonnement ; sophisme
false self soi artificiel
familial placing placement familial
family romance roman familial
fancy fantaisie, imagination
fantasise about (to) fantasmer sur
fantasy *(US)* fantasme ; fantaisie *(traductions récentes de Freud)*
faulty act acte manqué
feature caractéristique ; trait
feedback feedback ; rétroaction ; réverbération
feeding nourrissage
  feeding behaviour comportement alimentaire
feigning simulation
feral child enfant sauvage
fetish fétiche
fiducial fiduciaire
field champ, domaine
  field work recherche sur le terrain
figural after-effect effet Köhler
figure chiffre ; figure ; personnage
filler material matériel de remplissage
finger-thumb opposition pince
first-order representation représentation d'ordre premier
fissure scissure
fit crise, attaque ; ajustement
fitness *(darwinian)* valeur sélective
fixated fixe, fixé
fixation fixation
fixed (idea) (idée) fixe
  fixed action pattern (fap) séquence stéréotypée d'actes instinctifs
fixedness, fixity fixité
flashing exhibitionnisme
flattening rabattement
  flattening of affect indifférence affective
flexibility souplesse *(de structuration)*
  flexibility of closure souplesse de structuration perceptive
flicker papillotement
flight of ideas tachypsychie *(fuite des idées)*
flooding immersion
fluid intelligence intelligence fluide

flutter intermittence sonore
auditory flutter alternance sonore périodique
focusing focalisation
folium circonvolution cérébelleuse
follow-up (study) suivi ; (étude) longitudinale
following reaction tendance à suivre *(empreinte)*
food dispensing offrande alimentaire
foot-in-the-door pied dans la porte
forced compliance complaisance forcée
forebrain prosencéphale
forecast pronostic
foreclosure forclusion
foreconscious préconscient
foregrounding sollicitation
forensic psychology psychologie légale
formal operations stage stade des opérations formelles
fostering placement familial
fourfold point correlation coefficient r tétrachorique ponctuel
fragile person personne à risque
frame cadre
framework cadre ; bâti *(du visage)*
fraternal twins faux jumeaux
free association association libre
free-ranking classement libre
freedom of choice incertitude, liberté de choix
frequency fréquence; effectif *(stat.)*
fugue fugue *(épileptique)*
functional domination prépondérance fonctionnelle
fusion intrication ; fusion

G

gag reflex réflexe pharingé
gain (primary, from illness) bénéfice (primaire, de la maladie)
galvanic skin reflex/response réflexe psychogalvanique
gambler's fallacy faux raisonnement du joueur
gate control contrôle d'entrée
gating (sensory) filtrage (sensoriel)
gating mechanism mécanisme de vanne
gender sexe
gender identity identité sexuelle
geniculate bodies corps genouillés
geniculated tract faisceau géniculé
gestual imitation échopraxie
gestural gestuel
gifted doué *(enfant)*
glare éblouissement ; regard irrité
glia névroglie
glial névroglique
gloss luisance
glossolalia glossolalie
goal but
good enough mother *(Winnicot)* mère suffisamment bonne
goodness of fit qualité d'ajustement, conformité
grand mal épilepsie majeure *(haut mal)*
granularity grain
graph graphique
grasping préhension ; prise digito-palmaire
gregariousness grégarisme
grief chagrin
grip préhension
gross brut ; grossier
ground fond *(de figure)*
group dynamics dynamique des groupes
group fallacy illusion groupale
group test épreuve collective
grouping groupage, groupement
guidance soutien, tutorat, guidage
guide-line guide d'entretien
guilt culpabilité
gyrus (*pl.* **gyri**) circonvolution cérébrale

H

habit-forming accoutumant
habituation adaptation progressive ; accoutumance
hallucination hallucination
handedness manualité
handgrip pression d'empoigne
handling maniement *(du bébé)*
haphazard guess devinement au hasard
haptic tactilo-kinesthésique
hearing ouïe, audition
hebephrenia hébéphrenie
hebetic pubertaire
helplessness abandon ; impuissance *(à agir)*
herding grégarisme
heritage patrimoine
hindsight bias biais rétrospectif
histogram histogramme
histrionics théâtralisme
hoarding amassement, accumulation
holding soutien, maintien *(du bébé)*
home range domaine vital
homing retour au gîte
homophily effet de similarité
homunculus homoncule
horde of brothers horde primitive
hue tonalité chromatique
humour humeur ; humour
hypercathect (to) surinvestir
hypercathection surinvestissement
hyperesthesia hypersensibilité sensorielle
hyperphrasia logorrhée
hypnagogic hypnagogique
hypnoid, hypnoidal hypnoïde
hypnopompic hypnopompique
hypnosis (*pl.* **hypnoses**) hypnose
hypochondriacal hypochondriaque
hypochondriasis hypochondrie
hypothesis (*pl.* **hypotheses**) hypothèse
hypreresthesia hypersensitivité sensorielle
hysteria hystérie

I

iatrogenicity pathogénèse médicale
id ça
  id-relationship relation au ça
ideal ego moi idéal
identical twins jumeaux (homozygotes)
idiom idiomatisme ; idiotisme *(ling.)*
ikonic representation représentation imagée
illiteracy analphabétisme
illuminance *(US)*, **illumination** *(UK)* éclairement, éclairage
imageless thought pensée sans images
imaginal imagier
imagination imagination
imago imago
impairment déficience, déterioration
impediment empêchement, blocage ; troubles
imperviousness inaccessibilité ; imperméabilité
impingement empiètement
impotence impuissance (sexuelle)
imprinting empreinte ; imprégnation, fixation mnésique
impulse pulsion, impulsion ; influx *(nerveux)*
impulsion impulsion
inadequacy insuffisance
inborn inné
incentive incitateur ; motivateur, stimulant
incest barrier barrière de l'inceste
incidental accessoire, secondaire ; incidentel ; incident *(adj.)*
  incidental learning apprentissage *(acquisition mnémonique)* incidentel
incipient commençant
incitement stimulation, encouragement

inclusive fitness valeur adaptative globale
increased involvement hypersyntonie
increment augmentation ; incrément
incremental learning apprentissage progressif
independent variable variable indépendante
index (*pl.* **indices**) index ; indice ; indicateur
indicant indicateur
induce (to) induire, produire
indwelling installation (de la psyché dans le soma), sentiment d'habiter son corps
infancy petite enfance
infant nourrisson ; jeune enfant (qui ne parle pas encore)
infavoidance need besoin d'éviter l'échec *(Murray)*
infer (to) déduire
inferiority complex complexe d'infériorité
informal logic logique naturelle
infraconscious subconscient, infraconscient
ingroup groupe d'appartenance, in-groupe, endogroupe
inheritance hérédité, héritage
inherited hérité
inhibited inhibé
inhibition inhibition
inhibitory inhibant
inkblot test test projectif de tâches d'encre
innate inné
  innate motor pattern coordination héréditaire
  innate releasing mechanism (IRM) mécanisme de déclenchement inné
innateness innéité
inner self soi profond
inner speech langage intérieur
input entrée
insane aliéné
insanity aliénation
  insanity in pairs folie à deux
insensitiveness inaffectivité ; insensibilité
insight compréhension, intuition soudaine ; perspicacité ; insight
insomnia insomnie
instance exemplaire, instance
instinct instinct
(automatic) institutionalisation placement (d'office)
instruction consigne
instrumental décisif *(rôle joué)*, déterminant ; instrumental
  instrumental error erreur due aux instruments
intent (état d')alerte ; intention, but ; dessein
interaction interaction
  interaction process analysis classification de Bales
interdict interdit *(n.)*
internalisation intériorisation
intersubjectivity intersubjectivité
intertrial entre deux essais
intervening variable variable intermédiaire
interview entretien
  interview guideline guide d'entretien
  non-directive interview entretien non-directif
  semi-structured interview entretien semi-directif
intrinsic intrinsèque
intropunitive autopunitif
introvert introverti
invasive envahissant
investigator chercheur, expérimentateur
involutional melancholia mélancolie d'involution
ion pump pompe ionique
ionic channel canal ionique
isolation isolement *(thérapeutique)*
isophonic contour ligne isophonique
it ça *(Groddeck)*

J

jerk réflexe tendineux ; tressaillement
JND (just noticeable difference) seuil différentiel
JNND (just not noticeable difference) différence infraliminaire
job enlargement élargissement des tâches
joking relationship familiarité sociale
judge expert, évaluateur, juge

K

kainophobia peur de la nouveauté
katasexuality nécrophilie
kenophobia peur des espaces vides
key *(Skinner box)* levier réponse
kinesics gestuelle *(n.)*
kinetic cinétique
kinship parenté
knee-jerk reflex réflexe rotulien

L

labelling *(UK)*, **labeling** *(US)* étiquetage
labile changeant, instable
lag décalage
landmark point de repère
lapse lapsus
latency latence
lateral fissure scissure de Sylvius
leader chef, meneur, guide
leadership sens du commandement, qualité de chef, leadership
learned helplessness impuissance acquise, désespoir acquis
learning apprentissage
  rote learning apprentissage par cœur
legibility lisibilité *(présentation d'un texte)*
level niveau, modalité (d'une variable)
levelling *(UK)*, **leveling** *(US)* nivelage
lexicon lexique
liability responsabilité ; tendance
libido libido
life instinct pulsion de vie
like-dislike appétance-aversion
likelihood vraisemblance
  likelihood ratio taux de vraisemblance
link lien ; arc
linkage lien, connexion, enchaînement
linked associé, joint
lisp zézaiement
listenability capacité d'écoute
literature bibliographie ; documentation
litoracy oralphabétisme
loading saturation, poids ; chargement
locus of control contrôle (interne/externe)
log law loi de Fechner
loneliness isolement social
long-lasting/-term à long terme
longitudinal longitudinal
  scissure inter-hémispherique
look-say method méthode globale *(lecture)*
loop boucle
loudness sonie
lunatic fou
lunch decrement creux méridien

M

Machiavellianism machiavélisme
maladaptive inadapté
maladjustment inadaptation
malingering simulation *(de maladie)*
malpractice faute professionnelle, négligence *(médicale)*
managerial psychology psychologie du management
mania manie
maniac forcené, fou furieux *(n.)* ; maniaque, détraqué (sexuel)

manic, maniacal maniaque *(adj.)*
manic-depressive maniaco-dépressif
manifest content contenu manifeste
manipulandum objet manipulable
manipulatory intelligence intelligence pratique
marasmus marasme
marital therapy thérapie de couple
mark note
masking masquage
masochism masochisme
matched groups groupes appariés/de contrôle parallèlles
matching appariement ; égalisation
material matériel
maternal surrogate substitut maternel
mating accouplement
matrilineal matrilinéaire
matrix matrice, tableau
maze labyrinthe
mean moyenne *(n.)* ; moyen *(adj.)*
measurement mesure
median médiane *(n.)*, médian *(adj.)*
median deviation écart probable
medulla oblongata bulbe rachidien
medullary brain myélencéphale
melancholia mélancolie
membership appartenance
membership group groupe d'appartenance
memory mémoire
memory span empan mnésique
mental block blocage mental
mental defect déficit intellectuel
mental defective/deficient débile mental
mental retardation retard mental
mental set disposition mentale, état d'esprit
meridian trough creux postprandial
metarepresentational méta-cognitif, méta-représentationnel
microtremor micronystagmus
MID (**multi-infarct-dementia**) démence vasculaire
mid-collicular/midpontine transection encéphale isolé
mid-line system partie médiane du cerveau
midbrain mésencéphale
middlescence crise du milieu de vie
mimicry mimétisme
mind esprit
mirror image image en miroir
mirror phase/stage stade du miroir
misidentification fausse reconnaissance
MMPI Minnesota Multiphasic Personality Inventory
mnemic mnésique, mnémonique
mnemic decay déclin mnésique
mnemic store magasin mnésique
mnemonic mnésique, mnémonique
mnemonics moyens mnémotechniques
mode(l)ling modelage
monovular, monozygotic homozygote
monozygotic twins (MZ) jumeaux homozygotes
mood humeur
mood stabiliser thymorégulateur *(n.)*
moral grief douleur morale
morale (le) moral
morals (la) morale
motherese langue simplifiée adressée au jeune enfant
mothering maternage
motility mobilité
motion after-effect mouvement consécutif

motive mobile, intention, motif
motor function motricité
motor plate plaque motrice
motricity motricité
movement kinesthésique *(Rorschach)*
multi-infarct-dementia (MID) démence vasculaire
multiple personality personnalité multiple
multivariate analysis analyse multivariée
mundane realism réalisme ordinaire
muscle spindle fuseau (neuro-) musculaire
mute muet
mutualism symbiose
MZ (**monozygotic twins**) jumeaux homozygotes

N

nAch besoin d'accomplissement
nAff besoin d'affiliation
native indigène ; inné, naturel
nativism nativisme
nature-nurture debate débat inné-acquis
negation dénégation
neonate nouveau-né
nerve nerf
nervous nerveux
  nervous breakdown dépression nerveuse
nested sets ensembles emboîtés
neural neural
  neural network réseau neuromimétique
neuralgia névralgie
neurasthenia neurasthénie
neuroglia névroglie
neuronal network réseau neuronique
neurone neurone
neuropathy neuropathie
neurosis névrose
neurotic névrotique, névrosé
neuroticism névrosisme
neurotransmitter neuromédiateur
night blindness héméralopie
nociceptor algorécepteur
node nœud
noise level niveau sonore, fond de bruit
non-directive interview entretien non-directif
nonliterate (**culture**) (culture) non-écrite
non-REM sleep (NREM) sommeil lent
nonsense *(adj.)* sans signification
  nonsense word mot sans signification
noxa nuisance
noxious pénible, désagréable ; nocif, nuisible
NREM (**non-REM sleep**) sommeil lent
nuclear complex complexe/conflit nucléaire
null hypothesis hypothèse nulle
nurture «l'acquis», «nourriture» culturelle, éducation
nystagmus nystagmus

O

obedience obéissance
object objet ; but
  object relation(**ship**) relation objectale/d'objet
  object-presenting présentation de l'objet
objectivation objectivation
observer observateur
obsession obsession
obsessive-compulsive neurosis névrose obsessionnelle-compulsive
occupation profession
occupational psychology psychologie du travail, psychologie professionnelle
oculo-gravic illusion phénomène «des chevaux de bois»
odour *(UK)*/**odor** *(US)* **sensitivity** olfaction

Œdipus complex complexe d'Œdipe
old brain cerveau primitif
olfactory olfactif
one-tailed/one-sided test test de signification unilatérale
one-way mirror miroir sans tain
oneiric onirique
onset début, premier accès
  onset asynchrony asynchronie d'installation
ontogenesis ontogénèse *(particulière)*
ontogeny ontogénèse *(générale)*
open-ended question question ouverte
operant conditioning conditionnement opérant
operating characteristics courbe d'éfficacité
operational opératoire ; opérationnel
opiate opiacé
optic, optical optique
oral reflex (réflexe d')ouverture de la bouche
oral stage stade oral
order effect effet d'ordre/de position
ordinary devoted mother *(Winnicot)* mère dévouée ordinaire
organisational psychology psychologie du travail/des organisations
orienting response réaction d'orientation
outcome issue, résultat
outgroup hors-groupe, groupe extérieur, groupe de non-appartenance, autre groupe, exogroupe
outpatients' department dispensaire
output produit ; sortie
overachiever surréalisateur
overcompensation surcompensation
overdetermined surdéterminé
overflow débordement
overpopulation effect effet de masse/de surpopulation
overt ouvert, manifeste
overtraining surapprentissage

P

pædiatric pédiatrique
pain douleur, souffrance
paired apparié
  paired associates paires associées
palatability appétibilité
palsy paralysie
panel panel, type d'échantillon *(étude longitudinale) ;* groupe (de travail)
paracusis, paracusia paracousie
paradigm paradigme ; modèle *(théorique ou méthodologique)*
paradoxical sleep sommeil paradoxal
paralexia paralexie
paralysis paralysie
paranoia paranoïa
paraphilia perversion *(sexuelle)*, paraphilie
paraphrenia paraphrénie
parapraxis (*pl.* **parapraxes**) acte manqué, lapsus
parasexuality déviances *(sexuelles)*
parasympathetic parasympathique
paresis parésie
partial out (to) neutraliser *(variable)*
partile quantile
  partile division interquantile
path parcours, voie, piste, sentier
  path analysis analyse de parcours/des pistes causales
  scan path voie/parcours de balayage
pathetic fallacy anthropomorphisme
pattern modèle, pattern ; structure, schéma
pavor nocturnus terreurs nocturnes

payoff récompense ; résultat
peaking action de pointe
pecking order hiérarchie de dominance
peek-a-boo "coucou !" ; cache-cache
peer pair *(n.)*
 peer group groupe de pairs
percent hearing indice de reste d'audition
percept, perception perception
perceptual perceptif
 perceptual span écart oculo-verbal
performance performance
peripheral périphérique
permanent-object permanence de l'objet
persecutory persécutif
perseveration persévérance
personality personnalité
 personality synthesis bilan de personnalité
Peter Principle promotion jusqu'au niveau d'incompétence
petit mal épilepsie mineure
PGR *(US)* réflexe psycho-galvanique
phallic phallique
phantasied fantasmatique, fantasmé
phantasy *(UK)* fantasme ; fantaisie *(dans les traductions récentes de Freud)*
phantom limb membre fantôme
phase phase *(récurrente)*
phenomenon, (*pl.* **phenomena**) phénomène
phobia phobie
phonetics phonétique
phylogeny, phylogenesis phylogénèse
physiognomy physionomie
physiology physiologie
physique (le) physique
piagetian scales échelles de développement de la pensée logique
pictorial representation dessin
pilot study étude exploratoire
pineal body/gland épiphyse
pitch tonie ; hauteur
 pitch limit limite d'audibilité
 pitch residue résidu auditif
pituitary gland hypophyse
placement test test de placement *(classement, positionnement)*
plantar reflex réflexe plantaire
pluri-indebtness surendettement
pointer repère
poll sondage, enquête d'opinion
polymorphous perverse pervers polymorphe
pons protubérance annulaire
popular *(projective tests)* banal *(tests projectifs)*
population population
poster communication affichée
postpartum depression dépression puerpérale, baby-blues
postremity interférence proactive
postural sense sens des attitudes corporelles
posture position
potency puissance *(sexuelle)*
potlatch gaspillage ostentatoire
pre-conceptual phase phase préconceptuelle
pre-operational stage stade pré-opérationnel
preconscious préconscient
predictable prévisible
preferential-looking method méthode des préférences
prejudice préjugé
preterm infant prématuré
primacy primauté
primal primitive *(horde)* ; originel *(traumatisme)* ; originaire *(scène)* ; primal *(cri)*
prime amorce *(n.)* ; primordial, premier *(adj.)*
priming préparation ; amorçage
primitivisation régression
proband propositus, cas-indice

probe (to) explorer, approfondir, sonder
problematics problématique *(n.)*
procedure procédure
proceedings actes *(de colloques)* ; événements
process (to) traiter
process processus
processing traitement
product-moment method méthode des moments composés
profile esquisse, pattern
prognosis pronostic
projection projection
proportion fréquence
proxemics proxémique *(n.)*
psychasthenia psychasthénie
psyche psychisme ; psyché
psychic, psychical psychique
  psychic agency instance psychique
  psychic pain douleur morale
  psychic pregnancy grossesse nerveuse
  psychical research parapsychologie
psychoanalysis psychanalyse
psychoanalyst psychanalyste
psychoasthenia déficience mentale
psychodrama psychodrame
psychogalvanic reflex *(US)* réflexe psychogalvanique
psychosis psychose
  borderline psychosis prépsychose
  brief reactive psychosis bouffée délirante réactionnelle
psychosomatic psychosomatique
psychosurgery chirurgie du cerveau, psychochirurgie
psychotherapist psychothérapeute
psychotherapy psychothérapie
psychotic psychotique
pulse pouls ; impulsion acoustique
punishment punition
purchase acheter
purpose intention ; but
purposiveness intentionnalité
pyramidal tract voie pyramidale
pyromaniac pyromane

Q

Q-sort classification Q
quadriplegia tétraplégie
quantal discret, discontinu
querulousness quérulence
questionnaire questionnaire
quiet sleep sommeil calme
quota sampling échantillonage par quota

R

racial memory inconscient collectif
random aléatoire
randomisation variation aléatoire, randomisation
randomise (to) sélectionner/attribuer aléatoirement
randomness caractère aléatoire
range étendue, champ ; fourchette *(stat.)* ; variété
rank (to) ranger, ordonner, classer
  ranked ordonné
rank order ordre hiérarchique
rapport rapport
rate (to) noter, évaluer
rate taux ; rythme
  rate (of responding) débit de réponse
ratee sujet évalué
rater évaluateur
rating évaluation, estimation ; notation
  rating scale échelle de mesure, échelle d'évaluation
ratio rapport ; quotient, proportion
  ratio evaluation méthode d'évaluation

rationale raisonnement ; justification, explication
raw brut *(données, score)*
re-enactment abréaction
reach for (to) s'efforcer d'atteindre
reaching approche manuelle
reactance réactance
reaction *(adj.)* reactionnel
readability lisibilité *(facilité de compréhension)*
readiness état de disponibilité
reasoning raisonnement
reassurance rassurement
rebellious rebelle *(adj.)*
recall rappel
receiver récepteur
  receiver operating characteristic (**ROC**) fonction d'efficacité de l'observateur
recency récence
recognition reconnaissance
recollection recherche en mémoire
recovery rétablissement, guérison
recruitment recrutement
redesign (to) reprendre le plan *(expérience)*
redintegration réintégration
reducing capsule capsule oscillographique
redundancy redondance
reference référence *(bibliographique)*
reflection reflexion
regression regression
rehabilitation réadaptation, rééducation
rehearsal révision ; répétition
reinforcement renforcement
  adventitious reinforcement renforcement fortuit, aléatoire
reintegration réinsertion
rejection rejet
releaser déclencheur
releasing déclenchement
relevance pertinence
relevant pertinent
reliability fidélité, constance ; fiabilité, crédibilité
reliable fidèle, constant ; fiable, crédible
REM sleep sommeil paradoxal
remedial curatif
remembering souvenance ; (le fait de se) souvenir
repercussion retentissement
replicate (to) reprendre, reproduire *(expérience)*
replication réplique, reprise, reproduction *(d'une expérience)*
representability figurabilité
representational cognitif ; représentationnel
repress (to) refouler
  repressed refoulé
repression refoulement *(involontaire)* ; *(parfois, à tort :* répression volontaire*)*
repudiation forclusion
research recherche
residual rémanent
respondent répondant ; personne interrogée
  respondent behaviour comportement opérant
response réponse ; réaction
resting state potentiel de repos
restraint contrainte
restricted code code restreint
results résultats
retaliation représailles
retardation arriération, retard
retention rétention ; mémorisation
reticular formation formation réticulée
retina rétine
retrieval récupération, recouvrement *(mémoire)*
retrograde amnesia amnésie rétrograde
retrogression régression
reversal inversion ; renversement
review revue, compte-rendu critique ; historique *(recherches antérieures)*

reward récompense
rhinencephalon rhinencéphale
risky shift prise de risque
ROC (**receiver operating characteristic**) fonction d'efficacité de l'observateur
rod bâton, baguette *(tests)* ; bâtonnet *(rétine)*
role-play jeu de rôle
root conflict conflit fondamental, complexe nucléaire
rooting reflex fouissement
Rosenthal effect effet Pygmalion
rote learning apprentissage par cœur
rough model modèle approximatif
route-map parcours, itinéraire

S

sadism sadisme
sagittal fissure fissure inter-hémisphérique
salience relief
saliency saillance
salient saillant ; évident
sample échantillon
sampling échantillonage
  quota sampling échantillonage par quota
save (to) économiser
savings épargne
scale échelle
  scale analysis analyse hiérarchique
  rating scale échelle de mesure, échelle d'évaluation
scaling construction/utilisation d'échelle
scalogram board scalographe
scan path voie/parcours de balayage
scanning examen ; balayage
  biased scanning biais d'examen
scatter dispersion
  scatter diagram nuage de points
schedule planning, programme
schema (*pl.* **schemata**) schème, shéma
scheme combinaison, manigance ; projet
schizoid schizoïde
schizophrenia schizophrénie
  affective schizophrenia psychose dysthymique
scholastic backwardness retard scolaire
scholastic maladjustment inadaptation scolaire
scope portée
score note observée
scotomisation scotomisation
scribble gribouillis, griffonage
second-order representation représentation d'ordre second
sectioned confinement internement
seizure crise ; convulsion
selective reminding soufflage
self soi
  self-abasement dénigrement de soi
  self-actualisation réalisation de soi
  self-assertion affirmation de soi
  self-fulfilling prophecy effet Pygmalion, prophétie auto-réalisante
  self-fullfilment épanouissement personnel
  self-monitoring contrôle de l'expression
  self-preservation autoconservation
  self-rating auto-notation
  self-survey autopassation
semantic differential différenciateur sémantique
semi-structured interview entretien semi-structuré
senile dementia démence sénile
sense sens
  sense of (being) real sentiment d'être réel/du réel
  sense of guilt sentiment de culpabilité
sensibility émotivité

sensible sensé ; perceptible
sensitive sensible
sensitivity sensibilité
sensitisation sensibilisation
sensitise sensibiliser
sensory sensoriel
sensory deprivation privation sensorielle
sentience sensibilité
sentient sensible
sequela séquelle
series série
sex *(adj.)* sexuel *(relatif au sexe biologique)*
sexual sexuel *(relatif à la sexualité)* ; sexué
shading estompage *(Rorschach)*
shaping *(Skinner)* modelage
sheltered workshop atelier protégé
shibboleth signe d'appartenance
shift décalage
shifting changement ; inversion
shifting test épreuve de dominance oculaire
shock choc
sib, sibling (membre de la) fratrie
sibling rivalry rivalité de fratrie
sibship fratrie
SIDS (Sudden Infant Death Syndrome) mort subite du nourrisson
sight vue
sign-gestalt expectation structure signe d'anticipation
significant significatif
single-minded égocentrique
single-mindedness égocentrisme
sinistrality gaucherie *(le fait d'être gaucher)*
situation(al) psychosis psychose réactionnelle
sketch schéma
skewed asymétrique
skewness asymétrie
skill compétence ; habileté motrice
sleep onset endormissement
sleeper effect effet d'incubation
slip lapsus
slip of the tongue lapsus linguae
subordinate subordonné ; soumis
social social
social anchoring ancrage social
social control régulation sociale
socialisation socialisation
societal societal
sociopath *(n.)*, **sociopathic** *(adj.)* asocial
solid en trait plein
sorting classification
sorting test test de classement
span champ, empan, portée
span of control capacité de contrôle
spare épargner
spasm spasme
spectrum spectre
speech act acte de langage
speech therapy orthophonie
spinal cord moelle épinière
spine épine dorsale
split half method méthode de la bipartition
split-brain cerveau dédoublé
splitting dislocation *(des processus intérieurs)* ; clivage, dissociation
splitting of the object clivage de l'objet
spoonerism contrepèterie involontaire
spread étendue
spread of activation diffusion de l'activation
spreading diffusion
spreading depression dépression envahissante
sprouting bourgeonnement (nerveux)
spurt effort, augmentation soudaine
squiggle tracé (libre), ligne, trait
stage of object-love stade objectal
stamping-in/out effect effet d'impression
stance posture

standard étalon, modèle ; étalonné
standard deviation écart type *(écart quadratique moyen)*
standardise (to) normaliser, étalonner
standardised variable variable réduite
star as
startle reflex réflexe de tressaillement
statistical statistique *(adj.)*
statistics (la) statistique
status statut
stem stème
step étape
stepping marche automatique
stereoacuity acuité stéréoscopique
stereopsis acuité/vision stéréoscopique
stimulus (*pl.* **stimuli**) stimulus
stooge comparse, compère, complice
storage stockage, archivage
stored variables variables stockées
straight jacket camisole de force
strain tension
stream of consciousness monologue intérieur; courant de la conscience *(W. James)*
streaming répartition en «groupes de niveau»
stressor objet stressant
stretch reflex réflexe myotatique
striate cortex cortex strié
stuttering bégaiement
subconscious subconscient
subject sujet
sublimation sublimation
subliminal subliminal, infraliminaire
submission soumission
submissiveness docilité, soumission
substance substance ; consistance ; drogue
substitute substitut
substitution child enfant de remplacement
suckling nourrisson
Sudden Infant Death Syndrome (SIDS) mort subite du nourrisson
sulcus sillon
summation sommation
summoning attention attention prosexigène
superego surmoi
superiority complex complexe de supériorité
superordinate goal but superordonné/supra-ordonné
supine position décubitus
suppress (to) réprimer
suppression répression ; *(parfois, à tort :* refoulement)
supraconscious *(von Hayek)* supraconscient
surgency surgence
surrogate substitut
surrogate mother mère porteuse, mère de substitution/de remplacement
survey enquête
survey-map configuration
suspended attention attention flottante
symbol symbole
sympathetic (system) (système) sympathique
sympathy compassion
symptom symptôme
synapse synapse
synchroniser rythmeur
syndrome of doubles illusion des doubles

T

table tableau, table
taboo, tabu tabou
tabula rasa tabula rasa
tact *(Skinner)* réponse
tactual tactile
tadpole man bonhomme têtard
tantrum accès de colère incontrôlable
target cible
task tâche ; épreuve

task leader meneur de la tâche
TAT (**Thematic Apperception Test**) test Morgan-Murray
taxis taxie
temperament inventory enquête de personnalité
tendency tendance
test épreuve, test
achievement test test d'instruction
aptitude test test d'aptitude
completion test test lacunaire
equivalent test test parallèle
group test épreuve collective
inkblot test test projectif de taches d'encre
one-tailed/one-sided test test de signification unilatérale
shifting test épreuve de dominance oculaire
sorting test test de classement
test-taking passation
world picture test test du monde
testee sujet testé
thanatos thanatos
theoretical théorique
theory théorie
therapist thérapeute
they-group hors-groupe
thought blocking barrage mental
threshold seuil
tilting field champ oscillant
time out pause
timing chronométrage, minutage
tingling fourmillement
tinnitus acouphène ; tintement, bourdonnement *(d'oreilles)*
title titre
toilet training apprentissage de la propreté
token signe ; gage ; symbole
token economy économie de jetons
tone brillance sonore
tone burst/impulse bouffée de son
tone pip train de fuseaux de son
tone spindle fuseau de son
tonal brightness brillance sonore
topic thème, topique
topography ; topographical topique
totem totem
tracking poursuite
tracking eye movement poursuite oculaire
tradition-directed traditionaliste
training apprentissage, formation
training analysis analyse didactique
tranquiliser tranquillisant
transactional analysis analyse transactionnelle
transfer *(of training)* transfert *(en psychologie)*
transference transfert *(en psychananalyse)*
transient transitoire
transvestism travestisme
trauma (*pl.* **traumata**) traumatisme
traumatic (post-)traumatique ; traumatisant
trend tendance
trephinetrépan
trephine (to) trépanner
trial & error essai et erreur
trigger (to) déclencher
truth drug sérum de vérité
twilight state état crépusculaire
two-step en deux temps
two-tailed bilatéral
type-token ratio (TTR) rapport éléments/type *(ling.)*, densité lexicale

U

unbiased error erreur compensée
unconditional positive regard regard positif inconditionnel
unconditioned inconditionné
unconscious *(n. & adj.)* inconscient

underachiever sous-réalisateur
undexterity maladresse
undoing *(psychan.)* annulation rétro-active
unemployment chômage
unintegration non-intégration
unpleasure déplaisir
unsocial asocial
unstructured interview entretien non-structuré
utilisation time temps utile
utterance énoncé, énonciation ; émission *(vocale)*

V

vacuum vide
valence valence
validity validité
value valeur
variable variable
  stored variables variables stockées
variance variance
venereal disease (VD) maladie sexuellement transmissible (MST)
verbatim textuellement, mot pour mot
vicariation vicariance
vicarious vicariant
vicariously par procuration
viscidity viscosité
visile visuel *(n.)*
vision vision
visual visuel *(adj.)*
  visual cliff falaise visuelle
  visual speech langage visualisé
vividness attensité, vivacité *(couleur)* ; précision *(souvenir)*
vocal tract appareil phonatoire
vocational professionnel
voice onset time (VOT) temps d'attaque vocal
voltage-gated à ouverture électrique
voyeurism voyeurisme

W

ward département, service *(hôpital)*
we-group in-groupe
weaning sevrage *(nourrisson)*
weighting pondération
white noise bruit blanc
whole-word method méthode globale *(lecture)*
wholeness totalité
wiggling gigotement
WISC ; WISC-R **Wechsler Intelligence Scale for Children ; WISC Revised**
wish-fulfilment accomplissement du désir
withdrawal repliement sur soi ; sevrage *(drogue)* ; retrait
within-group intragroupe
wolf boy enfant loup
work therapy ergothérapie
work through (to) élaborer, perlaborer
working out élaboration
workload charge de travail
world picture (test) test du monde

X

X-axis (*pl.* **axes**) axe des abscisses

Y

Y-axis (*pl.* **axes**) axe des ordonnées

Z

zone of detectability écart/intervalle atonal
zooerasty zoophilie *(perversion sexuelle)*
zygosity type gémellaire

VOCABULAIRE FRANÇAIS-ANGLAIS

A

abandon helplessness
abandonnisme abandonment complex
aboulie abulia
aboulique abulic
abréaction abreaction, re-enactment
absolutisme absolutism
abstrait abstract
accentuation emphasis (*pl.* emphases)
accès de colère incontrôlable tantrum
accessoire extraneous, incidental
accolement au modèle closing-in
accomplissement du désir wish-fulfilment
accouplement mating
accoutumance habituation
accoutumant habit-forming
acculturation enculturation
accumulation hoarding
acheter to purchase
acides aminés amino acids
acouasmie acouasma
acouphène tinnitus
acousmie acousma
acquis acquired
  «l'acquis» nurture
acquisition acquisition
acroesthésie acroesthesia
acte act
  acte consommatoire consummatory act
  acte de langage speech act
  acte manqué bungled action, faulty act, parapraxis (*pl.* parapraxes)
  actes (de colloques) proceedings
action de pointe peaking
activation arousal
activités de déplacement/redirigées displacement activities
actualisation actualising
acuité stéréoscopique stereoacuity, stereopsis
adaptation adjustment
  adaptation progressive habituation
adapté adaptive; adequate; adjusted
adipsie adipsia
affaiblissement fading
affectif emotional
afférence afferent system
affirmation de soi assertiveness, self-assertion
âge d'acquisition educational age
âge réel chronological age
agénésie agenesis
agérasie agerasia
âgisme ageism
agrégat codé chunk
agressivité aggressiveness
aire d'audition auditory area
ajustement fit
aléatoire random
alexithymie alexithymia
algophilie algophilia
algorécepteur nociceptor
aliénation insanity
aliéné insane
altération fading
alternance alternation, alternating response
  alternance de codes code switching
  alternance sonore périodique auditory flutter
amassement hoarding
ambiance physique ambient physical factor
amendabilité capacity for reform
amnésie anterograde/de fixation anterograde amnesia
amnésie rétrograde retrograde amnesia
amorçage priming
amorce prime
analphabétisme illiteracy
analysant analysand
analyse analysis (*pl.* analyses)
  analyse aveugle blind analysis
  analyse de contenu content analysis

analyse de parcours/des pistes causales path analysis
analyse didactique training analysis
analyse factorielle des correspondances factor analysis of correspondence
analyse hiérarchique scale analysis
analyse multivariée multivariate analysis
analyse transactionnelle transactional analysis
analyste analyst
ancrage anchoring
ancrage social social anchoring
andropause andropause, climacteric
angoisse anguish, anxiety
anhédonie anhedonia
annulation rétro-active undoing *(psychan.)*
anorexie mentale anorexia nervosa
anthropomorphisme pathetic fallacy
antidépresseur antidepressant
anxiété anxiety
a(p)perception apperception
aphasie aphasia
aphasie de Broca expressive aphasia
aphasie fonctionnelle alallia
appareil apparatus
appareil phonatoire vocal tract
appareillage apparatus
apparié paired
appariement matching
apparition emergence
appartenance affiliation, membership; belongingness *(feeling)*
appétance-aversion like-dislike
appétibilité palatability
appliqué applied
apprentissage *(acquisition mnémonique)* **incidentel** incidental learning
apprentissage acquisition, learning, training
apprentissage de la propreté toilet training
apprentissage par cœur rote learning
apprentissage progressif incremental learning
approbation approval
approche adient behaviour
approche manuelle reaching
approfondir to probe
apraxie apraxia
après-coup deferred
aprosexie aprosexia
arborescence cluster
arc link
archivage storage
arriération backwardness, retardation
arriéré backward
artéfact by-product, artefact
as star
asapholalie asapholalia
ascendant ascendance, bottom-up
asémie asemia
asile asylum
asile d'aliénés bedlam
asocial asocial, sociopath *(n.)*, sociopathic *(adj.)*, unsocial
assaut d'idées brainstorming
assertivité assertiveness
association libre free association
associé linked *(adj.)* ; partner *(n.)*
assuétude addiction
astasie-abasie astasia-abasia
asthénie asthenia
astraphobie astraphobia
asymétrie skewness
asymétrique skewed
asynchronie d'installation onset asynchrony
ataxie ataxia
atelier protégé sheltered workshop
attachement attachment
attaque fit
attensité attensity, vividness

attente expectation
attention flottante suspended attention
attention prosexigène summoning attention
attrait appeal
attribuer to attribute
attribuer aléatoirement to randomise
attribution attribution
auditif *(n.)* audile
audition hearing
audition trans-crânienne cross-hearing
augmentation increment
augmentation soudaine spurt
autisme autism
autiste *(adj.)* autistic
autiste normal auto sensuous *(Tustin)*
autoconservation self-preservation
auto-passation self-survey
auto-notation self-rating
autogène autogenic
automatisme mental De Clérambault's syndrome
autopunitif intropunitive
autosensuel auto sensuous (Tustin)
autre groupe outgroup
avertissement *(Rogers)* awareness
avidité acquisitiveness
axe *(concret)* axle
axe *(abstrait)* axis (*pl.* axes)
axe des abcisses X-axis
axe des ordonnées Y-axis
axone axon

B

babil babble
baby-blues postpartum depression
baguette *(tests)* rod
balayage scanning
banal *(tests projectifs)* popular *(projective tests)*
barbiturique barbiturate
barrage mental thought blocking
barrière barrier
barrière de l'inceste incest barrier
barrière (hémato-) méningée blood-brain barrier
bâti *(du visage)* framework
bâton ; bâtonnet *(rétine)* rod
battu *(enfant, femme...)* battered *(child, wife...:)*
BDA (**bouffée délirante aigüe**) brief delusional disorder
bégaiement stuttering
bénéfice (**primaire**) (primary) gain
bénéfice de la maladie advantage by illness
besoin drive
besoin d'accomplissement nAch
besoin d'affiliation nAff
besoin d'attirer l'attention exhibitionism
besoin d'éviter l'échec *(Murray)* infavoidance need
besoin d'expliquer exposition need
besoin de performance achievement need
besoins vitaux dependency needs
biais artefact, bias
biais d'examen biased scanning
biais rétrospectif hindsight bias
biaiser to bias
bibliographie literature
bilan de personnalité personality synthesis
bilatéral two-tailed
bilingue bilingual
bilinguisme bilingualism
bionique *(n.)* bionics
blocage block, blocking, impediment
blocage mental mental block
boîte noire black box
bonhomme têtard tadpole man
boucle loop
bouffée de son burst of tone, tone burst/impulse
bouffée délirante aigüe (BDA) brief delusional disorder

bouffée délirante réactionnelle brief reactive psychosis
boulimie bulimia
bourdonnement *(d'oreilles)* tinnitus
bourgeonnement *(nerveux)* sprouting
bouton terminal end-button/-foot
brillance sonore tone, tonal brightness
bruit blanc white noise
brut gross
  brut *(score, données)* raw
  brut *(stat.)* crude
bulbe rachidien brainstem, medulla oblongata
but aim, goal, intent, object, purpose
  but super/supra-ordonné superordinate goal

C

ça id
  ça *(de Groddeck)* it
caché covert
cache-cache peek-a-boo
cadre frame, framework
  cadre comportemental behavior setting
cage d'activité activity box
caliginimètre dazzlemeter
calmant *(médicament)* ataractic
camisole de force straight jacket
canal ionique ionic channel
capacité ability
  capacité de contrôle span of control
  capacité d'écoute listenability
  capacité de sollicitude capacity for concern
capsule oscillographique reducing capsule
captativité attention seeking
caractère aléatoire randomness
caractéristique feature
  caractéristique distinctive distinctiveness
carence deficiency
  carence affective emotional deprivation
caresses sexuelles contrectation
cas-indice proband
castration, castration eviration
CAT Children's Apperception Test (CAT)
catégorie category, cohort
catharsis catharsis
cathexis *(Tolman)* cathexis
censure censorship
centrage centering *(US)*, centring *(UK)*
centré sur le client client-cent(e)red
cerebelleux cerebellar
cerveau brain
  cerveau dédoublé split-brain
  cerveau primitif old brain
  cerveau séparé bisected brain
cervelet cerebellum
chagrin grief
champ *(connaissances)* range
champ *(étude)* field
champ oscillant tilting field
champ visuel eye-span
changeant labile
changement shifting
charge de travail workload
chargement loading
chef leader
chercheur investigator
chiffre figure
chimiothérapie chemotherapy
chirurgie du cerveau psychosurgery
choc shock
chômage unemployment
chromie chromaticness
chronométrage timing
cible target
cinétique kinetic
circonvolution convolution
  circonvolution cérébelleuse folium
  circonvolution cérébrale gyrus *(pl.* gyri)
classe d'âge cohort

classement libre free-ranking
classer to rank
classification sorting
  classification de Bales interaction process analysis
  classification Q Q-sort
clinique clinic *(n.)* ; clinical *(adj.)*
clique clique
clivage splitting
  clivage de l'objet splitting of the object
  clivage du moi ego splitting
clôture closure
cluster cluster
co-jumeaux co-twins
cocher *(questionnaire)* to check
codage coding
code restreint restricted code
cognitif representational
cohérence consistency
cohésion cohesiveness
cohorte cohort
coït coition, coitus
coloration affective emotional tone
combinaison scheme
commençant incipient
communication affichée poster
comparse confederate, stooge
compassion sympathy
compensatoire compensating
compère confederate, stooge
compétence skill
complaisance compliance
  complaisance forcée forced compliance
complexe compound
  complexe d'inferiorité/de supériorité inferiority/ superiority complex
  complexe d'Oedipe Oedipus complex
  complexe nucléaire nuclear complex, root conflict
complice confederate, stooge
comportement behaviour *(UK)*, behavior *(US)*
  comportement alimentaire feeding behaviour
  comportement dissocié dissociative behaviour
  comportement opérant respondent behaviour
comportemental behavioural
composé compound
compréhension insight
compte-rendu critique review
compulsion compulsion
concept concept ; construct *(ex. test de Kelly)*
concluant conclusive
concrétude concreteness
conditionnement conditioning
  conditionnement des fonctions involontaires autonomic conditioning
  conditionnement opérant operant conditioning
confiance confidence
configuration survey-map
conflit fondamental root conflict
conflit nucléaire nuclear complex
conformisme grégaire bandwagon effect
conformité goodness of fit
confusion distraction
  confusion mentale clouding of consciousness
confusionnel confounding
confuso-onirique delirious
congénital connate
congruence congruity
connaissances techniques expertise
connexion linkage
connexité connectedness
conscience (state of) consciousness; conscience *(morals)*; awareness
conscient conscious; (to be) aware (of)
consigne assignment, instruction
consistance consistency, substance
consommation consumption
consommatoire consummatory

consommer consume
constance consistency, constancy, reliability
constant reliable
construct construct
construction d'échelle scaling
construction mentale construct
construit construct
contenu manifeste manifest content
contrainte constraint, compulsion, restraint
contre-investissement anticathexis
contre-validation cross-validation
contrepèterie involontaire spoonerism
contrôle (**interne/externe**) locus of control
contrôle d'entrée gate control
contrôle de l'expression self-monitoring
convenable adequate
conversion conversion
convulsion seizure
convulsivant convulsant
coordination héréditaire innate motor pattern
coordination intersensorielle cross-modal sensory integration
coordonnées trichromatiques chromaticity coordinates
corps calleux corpus callosum
corps cellulaires cell bodies
corps genouillés geniculate bodies
corps strié corpus striatum
cortex strié striate cortex
«**coucou !**» peek-a-boo
coupe transversale cross-section
cour courtship
courant de la conscience *(W. James)* stream of consciousness
courbe d'éfficacité operating characteristics
crédibilité reliability
crédible reliable
creux méridien/postprandial lunch decrement, meridian trough
crise crisis (*pl.* crises); fit *(nervous)*; seizure *(heart)*
  crise du milieu de vie middlescence
critère criterion (*pl.* criteria)
critique *(n.)* critique, criticism; critic *(person)*
critique *(adj.)* critical
cul-de-sac blind alley, dead end
culpabilité guilt
culture non-écrite nonliterate culture
curatif remedial
cybernétique cybernetics *(sing.)*
cyclothymique cyclothymic

D

daltonisme colour blindness
débat inné-acquis nature-nurture debate
débile mental mental defective/deficient
débit de réponse rate (of responding)
débordement overflow
début onset
décalage, décentrage decentering *(US)*, decentring *(UK)*, lag, shift
  décalage culturel cultural lag
décharge consécutive after-discharge
décisif instrumental
déclenchement releasing
déclencher to trigger
déclencheur releaser
déclin mnésique mnemic decay
déconnexion dysconnection
décrément decrement
décubitus supine position
décussation decussation
dédoublement de la personnalité dual personality
déduire to infer
défaillance failure

défaut fondamental basic fault
défense defence *(UK)*, defense *(US)*
déficience impairment
  déficience mentale mental impairment, psychoasthenia
déficit fonctionnel deficiency
déficit intellectuel mental defect
déflexion deflection
dégagement *(psychan.)* clearing
dégénérescence degeneration
degré degree
degré de liberté degree of freedom
  degré de séparabilité distinctiveness
délirant delirious, delusional, delusionary
délire delusion
  délire d'imagination delusional imagination
  délire d'un homme croyant s'être transformé en femme eviration
délusion delusion
démantèlement breaking up
démence sénile senile dementia
démence vasculaire multi-infarct-dementia (MID)
dendrite dendrite
dénégation negation
déni denial, disavowal
dénigrement de soi self-abasement
département *(hôpital)* ward
dépendance addiction
  dépendance émotionnelle anaclisis
dépendant addicted
dépistage detection
déplacement displacement
déplaisir unpleasure
dépression depression
  dépression envahissante spreading depression
  dépression nerveuse nervous breakdown
  dépression puerpérale postpartum depression
  dépréssion anaclitique anaclitic depression
déréel, déréistique dereistic
dérive drift
dérivé pulsionnel drive derivative
désadaptation de-adaptation
désagréable noxious
désamour delove
désapprobation disapproval
désaveu disavowal
descendant bottom-down
désensibilisation desensitisation
désespoir acquis learned helplessness
déshabituation dishabituation
désintrication defusion
désinvestir to decathect
désinvestissement decathection
désordre dysfunction
dessein intent
dessin pictorial representation
déstructuration destructuralisation
déterioration impairment
déterminant instrumental
détraqué *(sexuel)* maniac
deuil bereavement
développer to develop
déviances *(sexuelles)* parasexuality
déviation deflection
devinement au hasard haphazard guess
diagnostic diagnosis (*pl.* diagnoses)
diagnostiquer to diagnose
diencéphale between-brain
différence infraliminaire JNND (just not noticeable difference)
différenciateur sémantique semantic differential
différencier to differentiate
difficulté(s) d'élocution disfluency
diffusion spreading
  diffusion de l'activation spread of activation
dilemne dilemma
diminution abatement, decrement

diplacousie diplacusis
diplôme degree
discontinu, discret discrete, quantal
discriminant critical
discriminatif discriminal
dislocation (des processus intérieurs) splitting
dispensaire outpatients' department
dispersion scatter
dispositif apparatus
disposition mentale mental set
disséquer to dissect
dissociation splitting
dissonance cognitive cognitive dissonance
distinct discrete
distraction absent-mindedness, distraction
docilité submissiveness
documentation literature
domaine *(étude)* field
  domaine vital home range
donnée datum (*pl.* data)
double dual
  double lien double-bind
doué *(enfant)* gifted
douleur pain
  douleur morale moral grief, psychic pain
drogue drug, substance
duel dual
dyade dyad
dynamique des groupes group dynamics
dysfonctionnement dysfunction
dysharmonie cognitive pathologique cognitive heterogeneity
dyslexie dyslexia
dysthymie dysthymia

E

éblouissement glare
écart deviation
  écart atonal zone of detectability
  écart moyen average deviation
  écart oculo-verbal eye-speech/perceptual span
  écart probable median deviation
  écart type/quadratique moyen standard deviation
échantillon sample
échantillonage sampling
  échantillonage par quota quota sampling
échappement escape
échec failure
échelle scale
  échelle d'attitudes attitude scale
  échelle d'évaluation/de mesure rating scale
  échelles cumulatives confusion scales
  échelles de développement de la pensée logique piagetian scales
  échelon différentiel difference limen
échopraxie gestual imitation
éclairage, éclairement illuminance *(US)*, illumination *(UK)*
économie de jetons token economy
économiser to save
éducation education, nurture
effectif *(stat.)* frequency
efférence efferent system
effet effect
  effet consécutif after-effect
  effet d'ancrage anchor effect
  effet d'assombrissement dimming effect
  effet d'impression stamping-in/out effect
  effet d'incubation sleeper effect
  effet de génération cohort effect
  effet de masse/de surpopulation overpopulation effect
  effet d'ordre/de position order effect

effet de similarité homophily
effet Köhler figural after-effect
effet Pygmalion Rosenthal effect, self-fulfilling prophecy
effondrement breakdown
effort spurt
égalisation matching
égocentrique single-minded
égocentrisme egocentrism, single-mindedness
égoïsme egoism
égoïste egoist *(n.)*; egoistic *(adj.)*
élaboration working out
élaborer to develop, to work through
élargissement des tâches job enlargement
électro-encéphalogramme EEG
ellipse ellipsis
émission *(voix)* utterance
émotionnel emotional
émotivité emotionalism, sensibility
émoussement affectif blunted affect
(s')**émouvoir** to emote
empan span
empan mnésique memory span
empêchement impediment
empiètement impingement
empirisme empiricism
empreinte imprinting
encéphale brain, encephalon
en deux temps two-step
en pointillé dotted
encastrement embedding
encéphale brain
encéphale isolé mid-collicular/midpontine transection
enchaînement linkage
encoprésie encopresis
encouragement incitement
endogroupe ingroup
endormissement sleep onset
énergie cathexis *(psychan.)*
enfant de remplacement substitution child
enfant loup wolf boy
enfant reclus/du placard attic child
enfant sauvage feral child
engagement du moi ego-involvement
engramme engram
ennuyeux dull
énoncé, énonciation utterance
enquête survey, inquiry
enquête d'opinion poll
enquête de personnalité temperament inventory
ensemble aggregate
ensembles emboîtés nested sets
entraîner to coach
entraîner une réponse to elicit a response
entre deux essais intertrial
entrée input
entretien interview
entretien non-directif non-directive interview
entretien non-structuré unstructured interview
entretien semi-directif semi-structured interview
entropie entropy
énurésie bedwetting, enuresis
envahissant invasive
environnement *(visuel)* array
épanouissement personnel self-fullfilment
épargne savings
épargner to save, to economise ; to spare
épidémie epidemic
épilepsie epilepsy
épilepsie majeure *(haut mal)* grand mal
épilepsie mineure petit mal
épine dorsale spine
épiphyse pineal body/gland
épreuve task, test *(exam)*
épreuve collective group test
épreuve de dominance oculaire shifting test
épuisement professionnel *(syndrome d')* burn-out

équilibration balance
équilibre balance, equilibrium
équitable fair
ergonomie ergonomics
ergothérapie work therapy
érotisation eroticization
erreur compensée unbiased error
erreur de mesure by-product
erreur due aux instruments instrumental error
espace blanc *(tests)* blank
espérance (de vie) (life) expectancy
esprit mind
esquisse profile
essai attempt
  entre deux essais intertrial
  essai et erreur trial & error
estimation assessment, estimation, rating
estimer to assess
estompage *(Rorschach)* shading
état mixte bipolar disorder
étalon ; étalonné standard
étalonner to standardise
étape step
état crépusculaire twilight state
état d'alerte intent
état d'esprit mental set
état de disponibilité readiness
état-limite borderline
états affectifs affect states
étayage anaclisis
étendue spread, range
étiquetage labeling *(US)*, labelling *(UK)*
étude de suivi/longitudinale follow-up study
étude exploratoire pilot study
évaluateur judge, rater
évaluation appraisal, assessment, rating
évaluer to assess, to rate
évasion (d'une institution psychiatrique) elopement
événements proceedings
évident salient
évitement abient behaviour; avoidance
évoluer to develop
exact accurate
exaltation elation
examen scanning
excentrique eccentric
excitatif excitatory
excitation arousal
exemplaire instance
exhibitionnisme flashing, exhibitionism *(paraphilia)*
exogroupe outgroup
expectation expectancy
expérience experiment *(science);* experience *(life)*
expérimentateur experimenter, investigator
expert expert, judge
expertise appraisal
explication rationale
explorer to probe
exposition display
extérieur *(adj.)* extraneous
extraversion extroversion
extraverti extrovert
extrinsèque extrinsic

F

fabulation fabrication
facilitation facilitation
facteur factor
faillite bankruptcy ; failure
faisceau de nerfs bundle
faisceau géniculé geniculated tract
falaise visuelle visual cliff
familiarité sociale joking relationship
fanatique bigoted
fantaisie *(= fantasme)* fantasy *(US)*, phantasy *(UK) (in Freud's late translations)*; fancy
fantasmatique phantasied
fantasme fantasy *(US)*, phantasy *(UK)*
fantasmé phantasied
fantasmer sur to fantasise about
fausse reconnaissance misidentification

fausser to bias
faute professionnelle malpractice
faux jumeaux fraternal twins
faux raisonnement fallacy
  faux raisonnement du joueur gambler's fallacy
feedback feedback
fétiche fetish
fiabilité reliability
fiable reliable
fidèle faithful, reliable
fidélité reliability
  fidélité *(psychométrie)* consistency
  fidélité par équivalence alternate-form reliability
fiduciaire fiducial
figurabilité representability
figure figure
  figures intriquées embedded figures
fil conducteur clue
filtrage (sensoriel) (sensory) gating
fissure inter-hémisphérique sagittal fissure
fixation fixation
  fixation mnésique imprinting
fixe, fixé fixated
fixité fixedness, fixity
flux *(optique)* array
focalisation focusing
folie à deux insanity in pairs
fonction d'efficacité de l'observateur receiver operating characteristic (ROC)
fond *(figure)* ground
  fond de bruit noise level
force emphasis (*pl.* emphases)
forcené maniac
forclusion foreclosure, repudiation
formation *(lors d'un test)* coaching
  formation réticulée reticular formation
fou lunatic
  fou furieux maniac
fouissement rooting reflex
fourchette *(stat.)* range
(**sensation de**) **fourmillement** tingling
fragmentation chunking
fratrie sibship
frayage facilitation
frein cortical cortical inhibitory control
fréquence frequency
  fréquence normale baseline frequency
  fréquence normale d'occurence par unité de temps base rate
fréquence proportion
frontière boundary
fugue *(épilepsie)* fugue
fuseau (neuro-)musculaire muscle spindle
fuseau de son tone spindle
fusion fusion

G

gage token
gaspillage ostentatoire potlatch
gaucherie sinistrality, *(left-handedness)*
gazouillement babble
gazouillis *(de bébé)* cooing
genre *(ling.)* gender
gestuel gestural
gestuelle kinesics *(sing.)*
gigotement wiggling
glande surrénale adrenal gland
glandes endocrines endocrine glands
glossolalie glossolalia
grain granularity
graphique chart, graph
grappe cluster
grégarisme gregariousness, herding
gribouillage doodle
gribouillis, griffonage scribble
grossesse nerveuse psychic pregnancy
grossier gross
groupage grouping

groupe group, cluster, cohort
groupe (de travail) panel
groupe d'appartenance ingroup, membership group
groupe d'étalonnage criterion group
groupe de non-appartenance outgroup
groupe de pairs peer group
groupe expérimental experimental group
groupe extérieur outgroup
groupe représentatif cross-section
groupe sanguin blood type
groupe témoin control group
autre groupe outgroup
groupement cluster, grouping
groupes appariés/de contrôle parallèles matched groups
guérison recovery
guidage guidance
guide clue; leader *(person)*
guide d'entretien interview guideline
guider to coach

H

habileté motrice skill
hallucination hallucination
hallucination spéculaire autoscopic hallucination
handicapé disabled
hauteur pitch
hébéphrenie hebephrenia
héméralopie night blindness
hémiplégie diplegia
hérédité, héritage inheritance
hérité inherited
hétérozygote dizygotic
hétérozygotes élevés séparément DiZygotic twins raised Apart (DZA)
hiérarchie de dominance pecking order
histogramme bar chart, histogram
historique *(des recherches antérieures)* review
homogénéité consistency
homoncule homunculus
homozygote monovular, monozygotic
homozygote témoin co-twin control
honnête fair
horde primitive horde of brothers
hors-groupe outgroup, they-group
humeur humour, mood
humour humour
hypersensibilité/hypersensitivité sensorielle hyperesthesia
hypersyntonie increased involvement
hypnagogique hypnagogic
hypnoïde hypnoid, hypnoidal
hypnopompique hypnopompic
hypnose hypnosis (*pl.* hypnoses)
hypochondriaque hypochondriacal
hypochondrie hypochondriasis
hypophyse pituitary gland
hypothèse hypothesis (*pl.* hypotheses)
hypothèse nulle null hypothesis
hypothèse structuraliste *(Gestalt)* bundle hypothesis
hystérie hysteria

I

idéal du moi ego ideal
idée fixe fixed idea
identification apperception
identité sexuelle gender identity
idiomatisme, idiotisme *(ling.)* idiom
illusion des doubles syndrome of doubles
illusion groupale group fallacy
image corporelle body image
image en miroir mirror image
imagier imaginal
imagination fancy, imagination

imago imago
imitation par l'adulte de l'élocution infantile baby-talk
immersion flooding
imperméabilité imperviousness
imperturbable *(patient)* ataractic
implicite covert
imprégnation imprinting
impuissance *(sexuelle)* impotence
impuissance *(à agir)* helplessness
impuissance acquise learned helplessness
impulsion acoustique pulse
impulsion impulse, impulsion
in-groupe ingroup, we-group
inaccessibilité imperviousness
inadaptation maladjustment
  inadaptation scolaire scholastic maladjustment
inadapté maladaptive
inaffectivité insensitiveness
incapable majeur adult unsound of mind
incapacité disability
incertitude freedom of choice
incident *(adj.)*, **incidentel** incidental
incitateur incentive
incitation individuelle *(au jeu de rôle)* altercasting
inconditionné unconditioned
inconscient unconscious *(n. & adj.)*
  inconscient collectif collective unconscious, racial memory
incontinence fécale encopresis
incrément increment
index index (*pl.* indices)
indicateur index, indicant
indice clue, cue ; index
  indice de reste d'audition percent hearing
indifférence affective affective flattening, flattening of affect
indifférence du spectateur bystander apathy
indigène native
induire to induce
infirme disabled
infirmité motrice cérébrale cerebral palsy
influx *(nerveux)* impulse
infraliminaire subliminal
inhibant inhibitory
inhibé inhibited, inhibition
inhibition arrest
  inhibition d'aspiration aim-inhibition
inné inborn, innate, native
innéité innateness
insensibilité insensitiveness
insight breakthrough, insight
insomnie ahypnia, ahypnosia, insomnia
instable labile
installation *(de la psyché dans le soma)* indwelling
instance instance
  instance *(censure)* agency
  instance psychique psychic agency
instinct instinct
  instinct *(maternel)* drive
instrumental instrumental
insuffisance inadequacy
(non-) **intégration** (un)integration
intelligence artificielle Artificial Intelligence (AI)
intelligence cristallisée crystallised intelligence
intelligence fluide fluid intelligence
intelligence pratique manipulatory intelligence
intention intent, motive, purpose
intentionnalité purposiveness
inter-groupe between-group
interaction interaction
interculturel cross-cultural
interdit *(n.)* interdict
interférence proactive postremity
intériorisation internalization
intermittence sonore flutter
intermodal cross-modal
interne covert

internement sectioned confinement
interquantile partile division
intersubjectivité intersubjectivity
intervalle atonal zone of detectability
intragroupe within-group
intrication fusion
intrinsèque intrinsic
introverti introvert
intuition soudaine aha *(reaction, experience)*, insight
invalidité disablement
invention fabrication
inverse converse
inversion reversal, shifting
investigation enquiry
investir to cathect *(psychan.)*
investissement cathection, cathexis *(psychan.)*
  investissement externe exocathection
  investissement interne endo-cathection
  non-investissement acathexis
invoqué adduced
isolement loneliness *(society)*; isolation *(therapy)*
isotonie equal/equivalent loudness
issue outcome
itinéraire route-map

J

jeu de rôle role-play
jeune enfant (qui ne parle pas encore) infant
joint linked
journal diary
juge expert, judge
jumeaux homozygotes identical/monozygotic twins (MZ)
juste fair
justification rationale

K

khi-deux/-carré chi-square
kinesthésique *(Rorschach)* movement

L

labyrinthe maze
langage gestuel body language
langage intérieur inner speech
langage visualisé visual speech
langue simplifiée adressée au jeune enfant motherese
lapsus lapse, parapraxis (*pl.* parapraxes), slip
  lapsus linguae slip of the tongue
latence latency
leadership leadership
levier réponse key *(Skinner box)*
lexique lexicon
liberté de choix freedom of choice
libido libido
lien bond, link, linkage
  lien socio-émotionnel bonding
ligne squiggle
  ligne isophonique isophonic contour
limaçon cochlea
limite d'audibilité pitch limit
lisibilité readability *(comprehension)*; legibility *(text presentation)*
logique *(n.)* consistency
  logique naturelle informal logic
logorrhée accelerated speech, hyperphrasia
loi de Fechner log law
longitudinal longitudinal
luisance gloss

M

machiavélisme Machiavellianism
magasin mnésique mnemic store
maintien (du bébé) holding
maladie sexuellement transmissible (MST) venereal disease (VD)
maladresse undexterity
maniaco-dépressif manic-depressive

maniaque manic, maniacal *(adj.)*; maniac *(n.)*
manie mania
maniement (du bébé) handling
manifeste overt
manigance scheme
manque (de drogue) craving
manualité handedness
«Manuel statistique et diagnostique des troubles mentaux» DSM
marasme marasmus
marche automatique stepping
masochisme algophilia, masochism
masquage masking
matériel material
  matériel de remplissage filler material
maternage mothering
matrice matrix
  matrice croyance-valeur belief-value matrix
matrilinéaire matrilineal
mécanisme de déclenchement inné innate releasing mechanism (IRM)
mécanisme de vanne gating (mechanism)
médian *(adj.)* median
médiane *(n.)* median
médicament drug
méfiance fondamentale basic mistrust
mélancolie melancholia
  mélancolie d'involution involutional melancholia
membre d'une fratrie sib, sibling
membre fantôme phantom limb
mémoire memory
  mémoire photographique eidetic imagery
mémorisation retention
meneur leader
  meneur de la tâche task leader
ménopause menopause, climacteric
mère de substitution/de remplacement/ porteuse surrogate mother
mère dévouée ordinaire ordinary devoted mother *(Winnicot)*
mère suffisamment bonne good enough mother *(Winnicot)*
mésencéphale midbrain
mesure measurement
  mesure en facteur factor measurement
méta-cognitif/-représentationnel metarepresentational
méthode method
  méthode d'évaluation ratio evaluation
  méthode de la bipartition split half method
  méthode des moments composés product-moment method
  méthode des préférences preferential-looking method
  méthode globale *(lecture)* look-say method, whole-word method
mettre en valeur/l'accent sur to emphasise
micronystagmus microtremor
milieu environment
mimétisme mimicry
Minnesota Multiphasic Personality Inventory MMPI
minutage timing
miroir sans tain one-way mirror
mise en carte cognitive cognitive mapping
mnémonique, mnésique mnemic, mnemonic
mobile *(n.)* drive, motive
  mobile de réussite achievement motive
mobilité motility
modalité *(variable)* level
modelage modelling, shaping *(Skinner)*
modèle pattern, standard ; paradigm *(theoretical or methodological)*
  modèle approximatif rough model
moelle épinière spinal cord
moi corporel body ego

moi idéal ideal ego
monologue intérieur stream of consciousness
(le) **moral** morale
(la) **morale** morals
mort subite du nourrisson cot death, Sudden Infant Death Syndrome (SIDS)
mot pour mot verbatim
mot sans signification nonsense word
motif motive
motivateur incentive
motivation drive *(Hull)* ; motivation
motricité motor function, motricity
mouvement consécutif motion after-effect
moyen *(adj.)*, **moyenne** *(n.)* average, mean
moyens mnémotechniques mnemonics
MST (**maladie sexuellement transmissible**) venereal disease (VD)
muet dumb, mute
myélencéphale medullary brain

N

nativisme nativism
naturel native
nécrophilie katasexuality
négligence *(médicale)* malpractice
nerf nerve
nerveux nervous
neural neural
neurasthénie neurasthenia
neuromédiateur neurotransmitter
neurone neurone
neuropathie neuropathy
neutraliser *(variable)* to partial out
neutralité bienveillante benevolent neutrality
névralgie neuralgia
névroglie glia, neuroglia
névroglique glial
névrose neurosis
  névrose actuelle actual neurosis
  névrose obsessionnelle-compulsive obsessive-compulsive neurosis
névrosé neurotic
névrosisme neuroticism
névrotique neurotic
niveau level
  niveau sonore noise level
nivelage level(l)ing
nocif noxious
nœud node
non-intégration unintegration
non-investissement acathexis
non-usage disuse
normaliser to standardise
notation rating
note mark
  note en facteur factor score
  note observée score
noter to rate
nourrissage feeding
nourrisson infant, suckling
«nourriture» culturelle nurture
nouveau-né neonate
noyau caudé caudate nucleus
noyaux gris centraux basal ganglia
nuage de points scatter diagram
nuisance noxa
nuisible noxious
nystagmus nystagmus

O

obéissance obedience
objectif aim
objectivation objectivation
objet object
  objet manipulable manipulandum
  objet stressant stressor
observateur observer
obtention attainment
ocularité eyedness
oculomotricité eye movement

offrande alimentaire food dispensing
olfactif olfactory
olfaction odor *(US)*/odour *(UK)* sensitivity
onirique oneiric
ontogénèse ontogeny *(general)*; ontogenesis *(specific)*
opérationnel, opératoire operational
opiacé opiate
optique optic, optical
oralphabétisme litoracy
ordinaire *(adj.)* average
ordonner to rank
  ordonné ranked
ordre de contrebalancement counterbalanced order
ordre hiérarchique rank order
organisation consciente conscious scheme
originaire *(scène)* primal
originel *(traumatisme)* primal
orthophonie speech therapy
ouïe hearing
ouvert overt
(à) **ouverture chimique** chemically-gated
(à) **ouverture électrique** voltage-gated

P

pair *(n.)* peer
paires associées paired associates
panel panel
papillotement flicker
paracousie paracusis, paracusia
parade amoureuse courtship
paradigme (experimental) paradigm
paralexie paralexia
paralysie palsy, paralysis
paranoïa paranoia
paraphilie paraphilia
paraphrénie paraphrenia
parapsychologie psychical research
parasympathique parasympathetic
parcours path ; route-map
  parcours de balayage scan path
parenté kinship
parésie paresis
parorexie allotriophagy
partie médiane du cerveau mid-line system
passage à l'acte acting-out
passation test-taking
pathogénèse médicale iatrogenicity
pathomimie factitious disorder
patrimoine heritage
pattern pattern, profile
pause time out
pédiatrique paediatric
pénible noxious
pensée sans images imageless thought
penser to cognise
perceptible sensible
perceptif perceptual
perception percept ; perception
performance achievement, performance
périphérique peripheral
perlaborer to work through
permanence de l'objet permanent-object
persécutif persecutory
persévérance perseveration
personnage figure
personnalité personality
  personnalité multiple multiple personality
personne à risque fragile person
personne interrogée respondent
perspicacité insight
perte *(deuil)* bereavement
  perte de conscience *(coma éthylique)* blackout
pertinence relevance
pertinent relevant
pervers polymorphe polymorphous perverse
perversion *(sexuelle)* paraphilia
petite enfance infancy

peur de la nouveauté kainophobia
peur des espaces vides kenophobia
phallique phallic
phase *(récurrente)* phase
phase préconceptuelle preconceptual phase
phénomène phenomenon (*pl.* phenomena)
phénomène «des chevaux de bois» oculo-gravic illusion
phobie phobia
phonétique phonetics
phylogénèse phylogeny, phylogenesis
physiologie physiology
(le) **physique** physique
physionomie physiognomy
pied dans la porte foot-in-the-door
piège *(expériences)* blank
pince finger-thumb opposition
piste path
placebo dummy
placement assignment
placement (d'office) (automatic) institutionalisation
placement familial familial placing, fostering
plan design
plan d'expérience experimental design
planning schedule
plaque motrice motor plate
poids loading
point de référence anchor point
point de repère landmark
pompe ionique ion pump
pondération weighting
population population
portée scope, span
position posture
post-décharge after-discharge
postcure aftercare
posture stance
potentiel de repos resting state
pouls pulse
poursuite tracking
poursuite oculaire tracking eye movement
pouvoir classant discriminating power
précis accurate
précision *(souvenir)* vividness
précocité earliness
préconscient descriptive unconscious, foreconscious ; preconscious *(psychan.)*
préhension grip, grasping
préjugé prejudice
prématuré preterm infant
premier *(adj.)* prime
premier accès onset
prénatal connate
préparation priming
prépondérance fonctionnelle functional domination
prépsychose borderline psychosis
présentation display
présentation de l'objet object-presenting
pression d'empoigne handgrip
prestance *(éthol.)* display
présupposé assumption
prévisible predictable
prévision expectation
primal *(cri)* primal
primauté primacy
primitive *(horde)* primal
primordial prime
principe du tout ou rien all-or-none principle
prise de risque risky shift
prise digito-palmaire grasping
privation deprivation
privation sensorielle sensory deprivation
probant conclusive
problématique problematics *(sing.)*
procédure procedure
procédure expérimentale experimental paradigm
processus process
(par) **procuration** vicariously
produire to induce
produit output

FRANÇAIS-ANGLAIS

profession occupation
professionnel vocational
programme schedule
projection extrajection, projection
projet scheme
promotion jusqu'au niveau d'incompétence Peter Principle
pronostic forecast, prognosis
prophétie auto-réalisante self-fulfilling prophecy
proportion ratio
propositus proband
prosencéphale forebrain
protubérance annulaire pons
provoquer to elicit *(a response)*
proxémique proxemics *(sing.)*
psychanalyse psychoanalysis
psychanalyste psychoanalyst
psychasthénie psychasthenia
psyché psyche
psychique psychic, psychical
psychisme psyche
psychochirurgie psychosurgery
psychodrame psychodrama
psychologie psychology
  psychologie appliquée applied psychology
  psychologie de l'ingénierie engineering psychology
  psychologie des organisations organisational psychology
  psychologie du management managerial psychology
  psychologie du travail organisational/occupational psychology
  psychologie génétique/ du développement developmental psychology
  psychologie légale forensic psychology
  psychologie professionnelle occupational psychology
psychopathologie abnormal psychology
psychose psychosis
  psychose dysthymique affective schizophrenia
  psychose réactionnelle situation(al) psychosis
psychosomatique psychosomatic
psychothérapeute psychotherapist
psychothérapie psychotherapy
psychotique psychotic
pubertaire hebetic
puissance *(sexuelle)* potency
pulsion drive, impulse
  pulsion de mort death wish
  pulsion de vie life instinct
punition punishment
pyromane pyromaniac

Q

qualité d'ajustement goodness of fit
qualité de chef leadership
quantile partile
quérulence querulousness
question à double implication double-barrelled question
question ouverte open-ended question
questionnaire questionnaire
quotient ratio
  quotient d'instruction achievement quotient

R

r tétrachorique ponctuel fourfold point correlation coefficient
rabattement flattening
raisonnement rationale, reasoning
randomisation randomisation
ranger to rank
rappel recall
rapport rapport ; ratio
  rapport éléments/type *(ling.)* type-token ratio (TTR)
raptus attack
rassurement reassurance
réactance reactance
réaction response
  réaction conditionnelle/ différée delayed reaction

réaction d'éveil arousal
réaction d'orientation orienting response
réactionnel reaction
réadaptation rehabilitation
réalisation attainment
réalisation de soi actualising tendency, self-actualisation
réalisme ordinaire mundane realism
rebattu *(couleur d'objet)* dull
rebelle *(adj.)* rebellious
récence recency
récepteur receiver
recherche enquiry, research
recherche d'attention attention seeking
recherche en mémoire recollection
recherche sur le terrain field work
récompense beneceptor, payoff, reward
reconnaissance recognition
recouvrement *(en mémoire)* retrieval
recrutement recruitment
récupération retrieval
redondance redundancy
rééducation rehabilitation
référence *(biblio.)* reference
réflexe reflex
réflexe d'ouverture de la bouche oral reflex
réflexe de tressaillement startle reflex
réflexe myotatique stretch reflex
réflexe palpébral eye-blink
réflexe pharingé gag reflex
réflexe plantaire plantar reflex
réflexe psychogalvanique galvanic skin reflex/response, psychogalvanic reflex (PGR)*(US)*
réflexe rotulien knee-jerk reflex
réflexe tendineux jerk
reflexion reflection
refoulé repressed
refoulement *(involontaire)* repression*(sometimes mistranslated as:* suppression)
refouler to repress
regard irrité glare
regard positif inconditionnel unconditional positive regard
règle spécifique d'émission display rule
régression regression, primitivisation, retrogression
regroupement chunking
régulation sociale social control
réinsertion, réintégration re(d)integration
rejet rejection
rejeton (de l'inconscient) derivative (of the unconscious)
relation au ça id-relationship
relation au moi ego-relatedness
relation objectale/d'objet object relation(ship)
relief salience
rémanence after-image
rémanent residual
renforcement reinforcement
renforcement dépendant contingent reinforcement
renforcement fortuit/aléatoire adventitious reinforcement
renforcement secondaire/conditionné conditioned reinforcer
reniement disavowal
renversement reversal
répartition assignment
répartition en «groupes de niveau» streaming
repère cue, pointer
répétition rehearsal
repliement sur soi withdrawal
réplique replication
répondant respondent
réponse tact *(Skinner)* response
reprendre to replicate
reprendre le plan *(expérience)* to redesign

représailles retaliation
représentation d'actions enactive representation
représentation d'ordre premier first-order representation
représentation d'ordre second second-order representation
représentation imagée ikonic representation
représentationnel representational
répression *(volontaire)* suppression *(sometimes mistranslated as:* repression)
réprimer to suppress
reprise replication
reproduction *(expérience)* replication
reproduire *(expérience)* to replicate
réseau d'association association network
réseau neuromimétique neural network
réseau neuronique neuronal network
résidu auditif pitch residue
résonance intime *(Rorschach)* balance experience
responsabilité liability
résultat outcome, payoff; results *(pl.)*
rétablissement recovery
retard retardation
  retard mental mental retardation
  retard scolaire scholastic backwardness
rétention retention
retentissement repercussion
rétine retina
retour au gîte homing
retrait withdrawal
rétroaction feedback
rétrograde backward
rétrospectif ex post facto
réunir to collect
réussite achievement
réverbération feedback
  réverbération faciale facial feedback
révision rehearsal
revue review
rhinencéphale rhinencephalon
rivalité de fratrie sibling rivalry
rôle stéréotypé cultural conserve
roman familial family romance
rythme rate
rythmeur synchroniser

S

sadisme sadism
saillance saliency
saillant salient
sans signification nonsense *(adj.)*
saturation loading
savoir to cognise
savoir-faire expertise
scalographe scalogram board
scannographie Computerised Axial Tomography (CAT)
schéma pattern, schema
schème schema *(pl.* schemata)
schizoïde schizoid
schizophrénie schizophrenia
science du comportement behavioristics
scissure fissure
  scissure de Sylvius lateral fissure
  scissure inter-hémispherique longitudinal fissure
scotomisation scotomisation
secondaire incidental
sectaire bigoted
secteur catchment area
sélectionner aléatoirement to randomise
sens sense
  sens des attitudes corporelles postural sense
  sens du commandement leadership
sensation sensation
sensé sensible
sensibilisation sensitisation
sensibiliser to sensitise

sensibilité sensitivity, sentience
sensibilité (de tests) discriminating fineness
sensible sensitive, sentient
sensoriel sensory
sentier path
sentiment d'être réel/du réel sense of (being) real
sentiment d'habiter son corps indwelling
sentiment de culpabilité sense of guilt
séquelle sequela
séquence stéréotypée d'actes instinctifs fixed action pattern (fap)
série series *(sing.)*
sérum de vérité truth drug
service (d'hôpital) ward
seuil threshold
seuil absolu absolute threshold
seuil différentiel difference threshold, just noticeable difference (JND)
sévices battery
sevrage withdrawal *(drugs)*; weaning *(baby)*
sexe gender
sexué sexual
sexuel sexual *(sexuality)*; sex *(biology)*
signal buzzer ; display
signe sign, cue, token
signe d'appartenance shibboleth
significatif significant
sillon sulcus
similarité de son clang association
simulation malingering *(illness)*; feigning
sincère candid
sismothérapie electroplexy
social social
socialisation socialisation
societal societal
soi self
soi artificiel false self
soi profond inner self
sollicitation foregrounding
sommation summation
sommeil sleep
sommeil agité activated sleep
sommeil calme quiet sleep
sommeil lent non-REM sleep (NREM)
sommeil paradoxal paradoxical sleep, REM sleep
son binaural glissant binaural shift
sondage poll
sonder to probe
sonie loudness
sonnette buzzer
sophisme fallacy
sortie output
soufflage selective reminding
souffrance pain
soulagement alleviation
soumis subordinate
soumission submission, submissiveness, compliance
souplesse flexibility
souplesse de structuration perceptive flexibility of closure
sous-réalisateur underachiever
soutien guidance, holding
souvenance, se souvenir remembering
spasme spasm
spectre spectrum
stade des opérations concrètes *(Piaget)* concrete operations
stade des opérations formelles formal operations stage
stade du miroir mirror phase/stage
stade objectal stage of object-love
stade oral oral stage
stade pré-opérationnel pre-operational stage
stase *(libidinale)* damming up
statistique statistical *(adj.)*; statistic, statistics *(sing.)*
statut status
statut acquis achieved status
statut attribué ascribed status
stème stem
stimulant incentive
stimulation incitement

stimulus stimulus *(pl.* stimuli)
stimulus discriminatif cue-stimulus
stockage storage
structuration perceptive closure
structure pattern
structure signe d'anticipation sign-gestalt expectation
stupide dull, dumb
subconscient subconscious
sublimation sublimation
subliminal subliminal
subordonné subordinate
substance substance
substitut substitute, surrogate
substitut maternel maternal surrogate
sujet subject
sujet du même âge age mate
sujet évalué ratee
sujet testé testee
supposer to assume
supposition assumption
supraconscient supraconscious *(von Hayek)*
surapprentissage overtraining
surcompensation overcompensation
surdéterminé overdetermined
surdité deafness
surendettement pluri-indebtness
surgence surgency
surinvestir to hypercathect
surinvestissement hypercathection
surmoi superego
surnuméraire collatérale collateral sprouting
surréalisateur overachiever
symbiose mutualism
symbole symbol, token
sympathique sympathetic *(system)*
symptôme symptom
synapse synapse
syndrome d'épuisement professionnel (SEP) burn-out
synthèse abstract
système de croyances belief system
système nerveux central central nervous system
système nerveux végétatif autonomic nervous system

T

table table
tableau matrix ; table
tabou taboo, tabu
tabula rasa tabula rasa
tâche task
tachypsychie *(fuite des idées)* flight of ideas
tactile tactual
tactilo-kinesthésique haptic
taux rate
taux de vraisemblance likelihood ratio
taxie taxis
télencéphale endbrain
(**en deux**) **temps** two-step
temps d'attaque vocal voice onset time (VOT)
temps utile effective/utilisation time
tendance liability, trend, tendency
tendance à suivre *(empreinte)* following reaction
tendance à valoriser son rôle dans les événements positifs et le minimiser dans ceux qui sont négatifs beneffectance
tendance impulsive drive
tension drive, strain
tension artérielle blood pressure
tentative attempt
terminaison *(nerf)* ending
(à) **long terme** long-lasting, long-term
terne dull
terreurs nocturnes pavor nocturnus
test test
test arithméthique de rappel

digit-span test
test d'aptitude aptitude test
test d'instruction achievement test
test de classement sorting test
test de placement *(classement, positionnement)* placement test
test de rime clang association
test de signification unilatérale onc-tailed/one-sided test
test du monde world picture test
test indépendant de la culture culture-free test, culture-fair test
test lacunaire cloze procedure, completion test
test Morgan-Murray Thematic Apperception Test (TAT)
test parallèle equivalent test
test projectif de tâches d'encre inkblot test
tests parallèles alternate-form tests
tétraplégie quadriplegia
textuellement verbatim
thanatos thanatos
théâtralisme histrionics
thème topic
théorie theory
théorique theoretical
thérapeute therapist
thérapie de couple marital therapy
thymorégulateur *(n.)* mood stabiliser
tintement tinnitus
titre title
tonalité chromatique hue
tonie pitch
tonus alertness
topique topic; topography; topographical
total total, aggregate
totalité wholeness
totem totem
toxicomane addict
toxicomanie addiction
tracé *(libre)* squiggle
traditionaliste tradition-directed
train de fuseaux de son tone pip
trait feature ; squiggle
en trait plein solid
traitement processing
traiter to process
tranquillisant tranquiliser
transfert transference *(psychoanalysis)*; transfer *(psychology)*
transitoire transient
transpiration abondante diaphoresis
transversal cross-sectional
transversal-séquentiel cross-sequential
(post-)traumatique, traumatisant traumatic
traumatisme trauma *(pl.* traumata)
travestisme transvestism
travestissement cross-dressing
«trembleur» buzzer
trépan trephine
trépanner to trephine
tressaillement jerk
trisomie 21 *(mongolisme)* Down's syndrome
trisomique *(mongolien)* Down's syndrome
tronc cérébral brainstem
trouble(s) disorder, impediment
troubles de l'attention attention-deficit disorder
tubercules quadrijumeaux corpora quadrigemina
tutorat guidance
type d'échantillon *(pour étude longitudinale)* panel
type gémellaire zygosity

U

utilisation d'échelle scaling
(non-)usage (dis)use

V

valence valence
valeur value
  valeur adaptative globale inclusive fitness
  valeur sélective fitness *(darwinian)*
validation croisée cross-validation
validité validity
vanité egotism
vaniteux egotistic(al)
variable variable
  variable dépendante dependent variable
  variable dont l'effet ne peut pas être mesuré indépendamment de celui d'une autre variable confounding variable
  variable indépendante independent variable
  variable intermédiaire intervening variable
  variable réduite standardised variable
  variables stockées stored variables
variance variance
variation aléatoire randomisation
variété range
vécu *(n.)* experience
vérifier to check, to verify
vespéralité eveningness
vicariance vicariation
vicariant vicarious
vide vacuum
viscosité adhesiveness, viscidity
visée aim
vision vision
  vision stéréoscopique stereopsis
visuel visual *(adj.)*, visile *(n.)*
vivacité *(couleur)* vividness
voie path
  voie de balayage scan path
  voie pyramidale pyramidal tract
volée d'influx bundle
voyeurisme voyeurism
vraisemblance likelihood
vue sight

W

WISC ; WISC-R Wechsler Intelligence Scale for Children; WISC Revised

Z

zézaiement lisp
zone marginale borderline
zoophilie *(perversion sexuelle)* zooerasty

Imprimé en France par Europe Media Duplication à Lassay-les-Châteaux
N° d'édition : 001935-08 – N° d'imprimeur : 19472
Dépôt légal : juillet 2008